OFFERED

BILL R. MORRISON

WESTBOW
PRESS°
A DIVISION OF THOMAS NELSON
& ZONDERVAN

This book is a work of non-fiction. Unless otherwise noted, the author and the publisher
make no explicit guarantees as to the accuracy of the information contained in this book
and in some cases, names of people and places have been altered to protect their privacy.

WestBow Press books may be ordered through booksellers or by contacting:

WestBow Press
A Division of Thomas Nelson & Zondervan
1663 Liberty Drive
Bloomington, IN 47403
www.westbowpress.com
1 (866) 928-1240

For additional resources to use *Offered* as a part of your church ministry,
small groups, or personal growth visit www.OfferedAsWorship.com.

ISBN: 978-1-5127-4271-8 (sc)
ISBN: 978-1-5127-4272-5 (hc)
ISBN: 978-1-5127-4270-1 (e)

Library of Congress Control Number: 2016907955

Print information available on the last page.

WestBow Press rev. date: 06/06/2016

To Sheri,
always

CONTENTS

ACKNOWLEDGMENTS

This book is, in some ways, the product of hundreds of people. Dozens of public school teachers instilled in me a love for learning. I am especially grateful to Mrs. Phyllis Dunn and Mrs. Phyllis Jarrett, my seventh-grade English teachers. They were instrumental in teaching me the fundamentals of writing and developing in me a love for reading. I wrote dozens upon dozens of essays and read many literary works in their classes. Their dedication to being great educators will always be appreciated.

There are also dozens of faithful Christians who served in the churches of my childhood, Emmanuel Baptist Church and First Baptist Church of Moore, Oklahoma. Dedicated laypeople who served as Sunday School teachers and discipleship leaders modeled for me and for countless others what dedication to Christ looks like. Also, there was Rev. Paul Box, my only pastor from the time I was in fourth grade through high school. He was faithful to proclaim truth each and every week in his sermons. In addition, I was blessed by many college and seminary professors who taught me to understand the theology and truths of the Bible.

I have continued to be equipped during my adult years by several pastors, most recently Dr. Gary Fenton. He has been my pastor since 2000. I am especially indebted to him for mentoring me the past three years through monthly conversations over breakfast. His insights into leadership and ministry have aided me greatly in my ministry to college students. He also read portions of this book and provided valuable feedback.

I am thankful for the creativity of Jacob Pierce, a recent graduate of the University of Alabama at Birmingham, who was involved in Baptist Campus Ministries. He and my daughter Caroline worked with me to design the cover. Jacob is a frequent guest in our home, and he was a valuable sounding board for some of my ideas and thoughts in this work. Also, Lissa Handley Tyson was gracious to allow me to present some of this material in a series of weekly discussions. She gave valuable feedback and insight.

I am incredibly blessed to have been raised by two wonderful parents, Larry and Anita Morrison. Jesus wasn't just a "Sunday" subject in my childhood. They sought to weave faith into all aspects of life, which has served as a sturdy foundation for my life and this book.

I also give credit to my four children, Caroline, Annelise, Victoria, and William. The subject of this book has been discussed over breakfast and dinner many times for several years. They have given me their honest and forthright opinions and insights. When they responded, "That makes sense," I knew I was expressing my thoughts in a clear and understandable way. When they said, "Dad, that is hard to understand," it forced me to rethink the presentation of my ideas. Their feedback has helped in the communication of certain concepts contained in this work. Each of them has contributed to the makeup and biblical content of the book. They also gave me opinions on the design of the cover. A special thank-you goes to my oldest daughter, Caroline, who spent hours upon hours editing this work. Many e-mails were exchanged while she was studying abroad during the summer of 2015 and since then. Her English skills and biblical insights have made this a stronger book.

My biggest thank-you goes to my wife, Sheri. She is an amazing lady. I have been in campus ministry since 1988, nearly twenty-eight years, twenty-four of them married to her, and she has never voiced a complaint about the crazy hours I have kept, but always encourages me in ministry. Her role in our ministry has changed with the different chapters of our marriage and family. She is a fabulous hostess when students are in our home, a great helper when there are big events on campus, and a wise counselor to young ladies, among many other investments she has made in the lives of students. She is a true partner in ministry and wonderful companion in life. She also has given valuable input in the writing of this book.

There were countless nights when I would work late writing *Offered*, after everyone had gone to bed, and would leave papers, Bibles, and the computer on the kitchen table when I shuffled off to get some sleep. For weeks, there were dozens of pieces of paper with the commands of Jesus written on them scattered on the dining room table. Probably not the picture Sheri wanted to see each morning as she walked into the kitchen, but she supported my efforts, even when they were messy.

In different roles and with different avenues of influence, each of the people mentioned above have embodied the spirit and message of this book. For that, I will be forever grateful.

Bill R. Morrison

PREFACE

"Try harder." "Work harder." "Do better." "You should feel obligated to serve God more." Each of these phrases is—or probably has been—a part of our thoughts as we live our Christian lives. Each of them has at its core a common misunderstanding. They communicate that it is really impossible to live as Jesus wants us to live. It leads us to conclude we will always come up a little short. There is always something we should have done—ways we should have been more dedicated. These phrases are laden with guilt and regret. They lead to spiritual exhaustion.

They spring from a distortion of life and faith. We tell ourselves we must try harder in our Christian lives to make up for all the nonsacred or nonreligious things we do. This is completely opposite of the message contained in Scripture. We shouldn't think of our lives in terms of sacred and secular. Our lives and every role in them are either dedicated to Jesus or they are not. We can't make up for living part of our lives without regard to the will of God by serving God harder or getting involved in more things at the church. Neither do we earn the right to "indulge ourselves a little" in some secular pursuits because we have worked hard and have been dedicated to God in other areas. This kind of mind-set robs us and prevents us from living as He wants us to live—how He has called us to live.

Offered presents a clear alternative, an alternative that draws us to experience God as worshipers. It destroys the distinction between sacred and nonsacred. There only is worship of God or idolatry. In these pages, I hope you come to embrace the life you have been given as your unique expression of worship to the living God—the God made known by the living Christ. *Offered* will explore connections between the Old Testament and New Testament concerning worship and the Christian life. Apparent contradictions in Scripture will be explored that will be clarified in particular passages germane to the subject. The book is mostly devotional in nature.

I have written this as an offering of worship to God. I also offer it to you, not from a perfect worshiper but as a fellow worshiper. My prayer is that it is beneficial to your walk with God.

With warmest regards,
Bill

PART 1
THE TOTALITY OF WORSHIP

CHAPTER 1

LIFE IS WORSHIP

Life is worship. We never disengage. Worship is not a choice; it is what we are created for, and it is hardwired into who we are. We do have a choice, however, concerning whom or what we worship. The Bible gives consistent testimony that God created humankind to worship and glorify Him. Therefore, worship is the creative purpose for our very existence. To fully understand how God desires us to worship, we must move beyond the familiar expressions of worship that are so ingrained in our thoughts.

Powerful images and sounds flood our minds when we think of worship. We hear robed choirs with harmonies of fifty voices breathing life into age-old songs and hymns. We see neon lights spill between lifted, outspread hands, pulsating to a vibrating bass guitar. We feel the swaying rhythm of a gospel choir's passionate voices. We recollect a priest administering communion. We recall polite, stately men, passing offering plates to collect monetary expressions of commitment to God. We remember worshipful acts of reading Scripture and people kneeling in prayer. We hear preachers delivering heartfelt and heart-moving sermons. We may even think of professional athletes celebrating and pointing to the sky after a touchdown or a home run.

These are all valid and acceptable forms of worship, but they do not encompass all there is to worship. The challenge is to move beyond such limiting boundaries regarding worship. It is not restricted to that which takes place in a gathering of people specifically for a "time" of worship or as gratitude for an accomplishment. The expressions of worship listed in the previous paragraph involve a small percentage of our existence. God did not breathe life into us to exist only for moments of worship but for a life of worship. True worship envelops and encompasses the entirety of our lives.

So the natural next question is, what does a life of worship look like? The remainder of this book will answer this question by examining worship, who we worship, the person of Jesus Christ, and Jesus's commands and their importance in worship. On these foundations, several practical applications will be discussed, culminating in how we experience the ultimate expression of worship.

The beautiful part about God's creative work is that He created each person intentionally and uniquely. Therefore, the expression of your life of worship is unique and looks a little different from those around you. It is something each individual has the freedom to express to God, according to his or her call, within the framework of Scripture. Confining worship to designated occasions and narrow expressions leaves a large portion of our lives ignoring the presence of God. This happens because we do not have a clear understanding of what worship is.

Every person is at worship continuously through every role and activity. Worship is defined as offering any part of our gifts, talents, resources, passions, devotion, or leisure toward a cause, person, or divine being we deem worthy of our dedicated focus and commitment. Therefore, worship is not necessarily religious, but Christian worship is different. Christian worship is defined as offering all our relationships, gifts, talents, resources, passions, professions, and leisure to God, dedicating every resource, every role, every activity, and every relationship to God, acknowledging and embracing His continual presence and providence in every activity through Jesus Christ by the power of the Holy Spirit.

It is easy to live our lives without recognizing the scriptural truth that worship connects all aspects of our lives in a unified sacrifice to God. Rather, we spend our days compartmentalizing our lives by thinking religiously in religious contexts and secularly in nonreligious contexts. But there is no place in Scripture that allows for this disjointed view of humankind's existence in relationship with God. Everything we do that is not offered to God as worship is idolatrous and therefore sin. A person's life is either given to God in its entirety, or it is not. This is where we can fall into worshiping many things.

Within the different and the many, idolatry finds a foothold in our lives. Often, we switch between worshiping the one true God and worshiping one or more of the idols we have made of our families, friends, sports teams, jobs, status, wealth, and security, among other things. We forge these idols when we fail to see them as part of our consecrated lives of worship to God. How do we know if we have created idols? If we are involved in any of the above relationships and interests without presenting them to God, they are idols.

We construct these idols that divert and distract our worship of the one true God because we fail to grasp the fundamental concept that all of the previously listed things are not in competition with our worship to God but central to its full and complete expression. It is a challenge to give God the priority He deserves in our lives. When we see the nonreligious things in our lives as disconnected from our worship to God, this leads to the common mistake of trying to make God number one.

Christians identify this challenge of making God the priority that He deserves in their lives, and they try to address it through instilling commonly held mantras, such as "God is number one, family number two, and work or country number three." This particular hierarchical mind-set was popular in my grandparents' generation and evolved over the years. In the 1970s, during my teenage years, my church used "JOY—Jesus, Others, You." Today, my children are taught by some that they are second, and God is number one.

Notice the progression over four short generations. There was not any mention of the individual in my grandparents' generation, but the individual entered as number three in the 1970s. Now the individual ranks second. This generations-old effort to try to prioritize aspects of our lives in relation to God attempts to demonstrate His importance and authority. The problem is that although trying to help, these phrases actually obscure true worship.

There are good motives behind each of these constructs for organizing our thoughts and lives in relation to our allegiance to God; they testify to and indicate something elementary in our relationships with God—He is above everything. The common conclusion of each of the aforementioned statements is that they make God number one. This conclusion, however, falls short of biblical teachings and understandings regarding our God and His expectations and purposes for our lives. They veil the expectation of a total, unobstructed, and uncompromising worship of our Lord.

The practical outcome of such a bullet-point sequence of loyalties found in these constructs is that Christians get caught in the futile struggle of trying to live a balanced life. We engage in the impossible task of trying to square our lives between prioritizing worshiping God and doing the other necessary things in life to hold a job, raise a family, and take care of our own physical needs, among other roles and tasks. However, the key to a life offered as worship is not to prioritize God above all things but to dedicate each and every area of our lives to God as worship, for all that we have is a gift from God to be used in the fullness of worship.

Therefore, a full life is not a balancing act between our church and religious activities and our nonsacred involvements. We must be careful not to put the time we set aside for worship services and religious activities in a church on one side of a scale and put everything else we are obligated to do or enjoy doing on the other side of the scale, while trying to make sure the scale tips ever so slightly to the religious side. A balanced life championing church-centered commitments above all else does not validate us as good Christians. We do not live for the weigh in. In fact, this mind-set dangerously hinges on a works-based mentality. There is no scale. There is just a person whose heart and life is either still under his or her own control and possession, or there is a person who is completely the Lord's, dedicated to worshiping God through every aspect of life. God desires the person who is completely His, as revealed in the first commandment.

"You shall have no other gods before Me" (Exodus 20:3). I have heard some preachers and others misinterpret this commandment to conclude that God should be number one in our lives. The word translated as *before me* in the first commandment is from the Hebrew word *'al paniym* and literally means "in my face" or "in front of my face." *Before me* is not used as first in a numerical sequence, with God being number one, followed by a long line of things sequentially ordered behind Him. God is not part of a priority list: He is the focus and center of our lives. The first commandment means that nothing is to be in God's presence or sight, much like a minister at a wedding says, "We are gathered here before God and these witnesses." The minister acknowledges and brings the wedding guests to recognize that the covenant of marriage between a man and woman takes place in the presence of God.

When it comes to our worship of God, there is to be no other focus for our worship and nothing in the sight of God that claims any part of our devotion and allegiance. There is no one else in competition with Him. He is to be the sole recipient of our worship. He gives us breath in order to live in complete dedication to Him and His kingdom. We offer our lives as worship to the true God, expressed through spiritual stewardship of our lives. This is the worship God accepts.

Worship is our life in its totality—an offering of every role, every season, every chapter, and every endeavor. Worship through avenues and expressions that ignore this all-encompassing life of worship leaves a large portion of our lives as idolatrous. Therefore, worshiping God is not most important, not the number-one priority but the all-encompassing action. This calls husbands and wives, employers and employees, teachers and students, soldiers and civilians, and any other role or job we do to be offered as worship to God. This is the intent of Exodus 20:3 and allows us to fulfill "You shall have no other gods before Me." In chapter 18 of this book I will delve more deeply into these roles and jobs as they give life and breath to the first commandment. This kind of life expands our understanding and practice of worship far beyond the music in a worship service.

Beyond the Music

Preferences abound regarding worship styles in modern Christianity. These musical preferences have segregated modern worship experiences. Many churches draw a circle around the style of worship identifying local congregations. Some churches are known for a traditional worship style, complete with a choir, pipe organ, and piano, all accompanying the singing of hymns. Other churches are known for a gospel style of worship, with upbeat gospel songs much like those of camp meetings or the revivals of the nineteenth and twentieth centuries. Still other churches have a contemporary style of worship, replete with drums, electric guitars, acoustic guitars, and electric keyboards. Some churches have a mixture of two or three different genres of music and incorporate musical instrumentation across these differing styles.

Regardless of the style used by a particular church, some people stake out territory, even calling into question one's fervency in spreading the gospel or one's spiritual depth, based on musical preferences. We've all heard of it happening—churches split, congregations wounded, and people hurt over the musical styles used in worship. It's ironic that one of the primary demonstrations of unity and fellowship for a Christian church has created so many divisions and judgmental attitudes over the past few decades. The probable cause of such fervently held positions regarding music in worship is a fundamental misunderstanding and improper practice of what complete worship encompasses.

We are in a day where denominational affiliations are diminishing. We are not as segmented in our churches by the names Baptist, Catholic, Episcopal, Lutheran, Methodist, Pentecostal, or Presbyterian. But we have left one set of labels and distinctions and embraced another set of differences. Individual churches now are identified by worship style as much as—if not more than—denominational affiliations. There seems to be as big a dividing line developing in the twenty-first century as there was in the previous five centuries, with just different criteria for the division. An entirely new branch of the church is emerging, and almost without exception, it is identified with one tradition of worship.

The nondenominational, or community church has gained increasing prominence in American society, and it almost exclusively expresses a contemporary worship style. Many old-line churches affiliated with a denomination have adopted the same contemporary style of music. There is absolutely nothing wrong with or unbiblical about a contemporary style of worship. In fact, it is a beautiful demonstration of people offering their passions and talents to God as worship, just as those who worship through more traditional expressions of music offer their passions and talents to God as worship. Many Christians choose a church based on the musical styles expressed in a worship service. The risk in giving so much attention to the structure and form of worship is that we may overlook one essential question: what does God desire in the broader context of worship?

When churches or Christians make a worship style their primary identity, it can facilitate a shallow spirituality that allows Christians to minimize or ignore the most devoted form of worship—a consecrated life. Neither contemporary nor traditional instrumentation used in church worship services ushers in any more of the presence of God than the other. Matthew 18:20 states, "For where two or three have gathered together in My name, I am there in their midst." We can conclude that Jesus's presence is real in any worship service in a church, regardless of the musical style, as long as two or more have gathered in His name. We worship this God who is present with us without divided loyalties.

The second commandment is, "You shall not make for yourself an idol, or any likeness of what is in heaven above or on the earth beneath or in the water under the earth" (Exodus 20:4). The Israelites were not allowed to have anything in their lives that competed with their full worship of Yahweh, even if it was a representation of something beautiful or good—something God created. They were expected to dedicate their lives to God alone, not reserve some things that had special meaning for them in place of their commitment to God. Alternating between commitments places parts of our lives in competition with God. This allows us to avoid the necessary work of seeking how every aspect of our lives is to be devoted to God. He is not a god among other things—He is God alone.

Switching our commitment between God and people, hobbies and interests, instead of committing these things to God through our relationship with Him, is the modern practice of idolatry. When we give God only certain parts of our lives but reserve a special place in our hearts and lives for the other parts, we, in effect, worship idols. God, however, gives every aspect of our lives meaning when they are dedicated to Him and His purposes. God calls us to complete allegiance, as He clearly expresses in the first and second commandments. Anything other than this type of worship is idolatrous because it allows other things to compete with God.

It may seem odd to use the words *idolatrous* and *worship* in the same sentence, but corporate and private worship is idolatrous if it is directed toward ourselves or fails to encompass the entire picture of worship as found in the teachings of the Bible; this includes the Law, prophets, and Gospels. Worship was never to be identified solely by place or style but through who we are, who we are becoming, and who we are following. When we do this, worship becomes the totality of our human existence and experience in God. Attempting to split time between sacred and nonsacred involvements is disastrous for spiritual vitality. We have to move beyond the music to discover that for which we were created.

Created for Worship

God doesn't just demand worship ambiguously, but He created humankind with intentional roles to express worship. Heavenly creatures also have been given roles in worship. The glimpses of heaven we see in Scripture describe a societal structure, with angels fulfilling roles of worship in the celestial realm. We get a glimpse of heaven in Isaiah 6, as the prophet gives a description of angels singing praises to God in His very presence. Similarly, humanity possesses avenues to bestow expressions of worship.

In Genesis, God gives Adam the task of naming each of the animals. Adam and Eve also receive the vocation of tending creation, which was a part of their daily sacrifice of worship to God. These tasks were a high calling, not menial work. The fulfillment of these roles pleased God, for His creation spoke of and demonstrated His glory. The humans' call and work, as God's trusted stewards, was a privilege—the first vocation. God gave them the honor and opportunity to care for that which He highly esteemed. This daily tending to and enjoyment of God's creation culminated in a personal encounter with God in the evening, the ultimate close to a day lived fulfilling God's will and purpose (Genesis 3:8).

Genesis also indicates how our labors are an expression of worship through the story of Cain and Abel. These two brothers brought the fruit of their labor, one tending the ground and one tending the flocks, as an offering to God. However, God accepted Abel's offering and rejected Cain's (Genesis 4:1–8). God did not reject Cain's offering merely because it was produce, because there are grain offerings and other food offerings prescribed in the Law. Although the Genesis passage is not as clear about the reasons that Cain's offering was rejected by God and why Cain killed his brother, 1 John 3:12 states, "Cain, who was of the evil one and slew his brother. And for what reason did he slay him? Because his deeds were evil, and his brother's were righteous."

This leads us to conclude that God rejected Cain's sacrifice because Cain lived an unrighteous life and harbored hatred in his heart, which is revealed by his reaction to God and Abel when God rejected his sacrifice. Cain's response should have been to repent, seek God's will, and ask God to change his heart. Instead, Cain responded by murdering his brother, an act already prepared in his heart because of a lack of concern for Abel, as evidenced by the question "Am I my brother's keeper?" (Genesis 4:9). This story speaks to the truth that our expressions of worship must first originate from a heart that is touched and transformed by God and a life that is dedicated in its worship of God—a life of faith.

Cain's offering was flawed, not because of what it was but because of his unrighteous life and the content of his heart—a heart that was unveiled to expose its hatred and anger. Abel's offering was accepted, not merely because of what it was but because of his righteous life and the content of his heart. "By faith Abel offered to God a better sacrifice than Cain, through which he obtained the testimony that he was righteous" (Hebrews 11:4). When we worship God from a self-determined and self-defined heart, we are not involved in biblical worship but are trapped in an attempted manipulation of God through merely outward signs of religion.

All humans are in a continual state of worship. The question is, do our lives demonstrate worship of the true God, or do they demonstrate worship of a god of our own making? If it is a god of our own making, we will never experience worship of God in spirit and truth; instead, we will be hopelessly lost in an unfulfilling, unquenchable thirst—in life and in every worship experience, regardless of whether it meets our predisposed expectations. Our expectations, shaped by the modern world, lead us away from the notion and practice that worship is connected to sacrifice. Yet we know from many passages in the Bible that worship and sacrifice are intimately connected in the Old Testament Law and in the life of Jesus, even if not in the way we assume they are.

CHAPTER 2

OFFERED AS WORSHIP

The Offered Life

Our lives are offered as worship. The concept is not complicated; in fact, it is surprisingly simple but life-altering and life-encompassing in its scope. This phrase "offered as worship" impacts every area of our existence and every role we have in life. Romans 12:1–2 states, "Therefore I urge you, brethren, by the mercies of God, to present your bodies a living and holy sacrifice, acceptable to God, which is your spiritual service of worship. And do not be conformed to this world, but be transformed by the renewing of your mind, so that you may prove what the will of God is, that which is good and acceptable and perfect." This passage of Scripture is the ultimate life principle, birthed from Paul's extensive explanation of revelation, sin, election, and salvation by grace, found in the book of Romans.

The Greek word translated "service of worship" in Romans 12:1 is *latreian*. The corresponding word in Hebrew is *abodah* and when used in the Old Testament in the context of worship is translated as "the service of the Lord" (2 Chronicles 35:16; cf. Numbers 8:11, Joshua 22:27). Paul understood that "worship" and "service" are inseparable. Many Christians point to passages in Romans that address predestination and election as the central teachings in Romans. Paul's prevalent and commonly overlooked focus, however, is on worship—a life of worship. The essence of life for the apostle Paul was offering his life as worship through sacrifice.

Sacrifice is Central to Worship

Sacrifice is a central theme of the Old Testament. The word *sacrifice* immediately draws a Christian's mind to the Old Testament sacrificial system. In Numbers 29:2, the sacrifices are called burnt offerings. Also, the books of Exodus and Leviticus explain an elaborate system of sacrifice. People made sacrifices for atonement, burnt offerings, sin offerings, peace offerings, and guilt offerings, among others. Worship through the sacrificial system resulted in many things, including communion, confession, and atonement. Sacrifices were gifts to God. Sacrifices of atonement covered people's sins. By the end of the Old Testament period, all sacrifices were believed to have atoning value.[1]

In Exodus 29:38–46, the nation is instructed to sacrifice a lamb with a grain offering and drink offering each morning and at twilight. The fine flower, beaten oil, and wine was to be offered with the lambs as burnt offerings to the Lord. This sacrifice of a lamb, grain, and drink offering was to continue throughout the generations—each and every day. It was "for a soothing aroma, an offering by fire to the Lord. It shall be a continual burnt offering throughout your generations at the doorway of the tent of meeting before the Lord" (Exodus 29:41–42).

In other words, the nation of Israel was to be in a continual state of worship through the animal sacrifices offered by the priests in the Tabernacle and, later, Temple. Worship was to never cease throughout the entire future of the nation of Israel. God promises

---

[1] C. R. North, "Sacrifice," *A Theological Word Book of the Bible,* ed. Alan Richardson (New York: Macmillan Publishing Co., Inc., 1950), 206.

His presence to Israel in the midst of these continual sacrifices. Exodus 29:42 ends with "where I will meet with you, to speak to you there." The purpose of these twice-daily sacrifices was to signify that the nation was living in sacrifice, and through that sacrifice, God meets with them and speaks to them. Sacrifice brings communion with God—fellowship with Him. It is through this offering of worship that God speaks to His children, blessing them with His presence and guiding their lives. Two significant insights into these sacrifices are important to the Christian in daily living.

First, a life of sacrifice is not to be lived out of guilt for our past sins or out of obligation for having been blessed. It does not matter how wealthy we are or how poor we are. God gave everyone the same calling to be His follower—a call to sacrifice our lives in their totality. The rich should not feel obligated to give to the poor or to do missions because they live in abundance, wealthy ZIP codes, or secure areas. We give to the poor and do missions because of what Christ has done in us—because of our changed hearts. This is living in freedom.

Second, when we become Christians, we are to offer a continuous sacrifice of worship to our God. I love the phrase, "It shall be a continual burnt offering throughout your generations" (Exodus 29:42). This, coupled with Paul's instruction in Romans 12:1 to present our bodies a living sacrifice, is the inspiration to be the living, ongoing, never-ending sacrifice expected of the followers of Jesus. We sacrifice our lives entirely on the altar of worship. Dying physically for the faith is not something we seek or strive for as proof of our commitment. Nor is it required of or does it happen to the vast majority of Christians, but if it happens it will come as a result of how we live in Christ.

It may seem odd, but martyrs for the Christian faith have already been dying. They have embodied the call to offer their lives as worship by dying to themselves. We are all called to martyrdom; some will die a physical death as a result of being a Christian, while everyone else dies daily to self through a lifelong and long life of sacrificial love. This mind-set and commitment must be a part of the foundation of offering our lives as worship to God. We, the believers in Jesus as Lord and Savior, are the living sacrifice in companionship with the living God, in the power of the risen, living Lord. This living sacrifice, our lives offered as worship, is the expression and witness of God to the world. This type of sacrifice is also seen in other places in the Old Testament.

True Worship in the Old Testament

In Leviticus 23:21, the nation of Israel is commanded to have a sacred assembly. There are also elaborate instructions about sacrifice found in Leviticus. In Psalm 100, Israel is told to join the entire earth in shouting praise to God. A great deal of the Old Testament sets forth a very intricate worship system. All of this comes about to help the nation of Israel fulfill the first two commandments, which we have established address worship and idolatry (Exodus 20:1–4).

However, through the prophet Amos, God says,

> "I hate, I reject your festivals, Nor do I delight in your solemn assemblies. Even though you offer up to Me burnt offerings and your grain offerings, I will not accept them; and I will not even look at the peace offerings of your fatlings. Take away from me the noise of your songs; I will not even listen to the sound of your harps. But let justice roll down like waters and righteousness like an ever-flowing stream" (Amos 5:21–24).

Taken at face value, Leviticus 23:21 and Amos 5:21–24 stand in contradiction to one another. Leviticus 23:21 commands the children of Israel to hold a solemn assembly, while Amos 5:21–24 states that God rejects a solemn assembly. God dismissed the sacrificial system, festivals, solemn assemblies, and corporate worship in one brief prophesy by Amos. So what's the point? Do we throw our hands up and say, "It's hopeless; there is no way to please God. No matter what we do, it will be wrong"? Did God mean what He said in Leviticus or what He said in the book of Amos? Has God somehow changed what He views as acceptable worship? Not at all. God is consistent.

The sacrificial system, festivals, solemn assemblies, and corporate worship mentioned in the Law were to be a testimony of an already committed and consecrated daily life. They were not to be done in place of a daily life of commitment to God. A consecrated life, offered and completely devoted to God, must be present for our corporate worship to be accepted by Him. By the time Amos was written, it is evident that the forms of public worship were used as merely a religious statement, not a faith commitment.

What the people had lost in all the commands about religious festivals and solemn assemblies—those special times of worship—is the reason God set His people apart from other nations. The instructions in Leviticus are predicated upon the children of Israel living a holy life—a life consecrated and set apart. They were to be different from the nations around them. Israel was to be a blessing to the nations—a light to the nations, extolling the love of God for all people, as seen when God promised Abraham in Genesis 12:2, "And I will make you a great nation, And I will bless you, and make your name great, And so you shall be a blessing."

Yahweh, the only true God, desired to demonstrate His power and love to humanity through Israel and set her aside for these purposes. This can be seen in the twenty-third chapter of Leviticus. Leviticus 23:1–21 and 23:23–44 deal with sacrifices and festivals. In the middle of all the instructions about public worship was a command—one verse—that touched the intent of the commands given to the people concerning worship. It says, "When you reap the harvest of your land, moreover, you shall not reap to the very corners of your field nor gather the gleaning of your harvest; you are to leave them for the needy and the alien. I am the Lord your God" (Leviticus 23:22).

Verse 22 seems out of place at first reading, but upon further examination, it is the most poignant verse in Leviticus 23. Israel's worship was always to envelop people with love and concern, especially the needy, who cannot provide for themselves, including the immigrants, who were trying to begin a new life. Our gathered worship is not at the expense of God's love and provision for humankind but is central to it. This has never changed, but God's children do occasionally change.

By the time of Amos, the sin was not just neglect of the poor but intentional abuse of the poor through the courts. "For I know your transgressions are many and your sins are great, You who distress the righteous and accept bribes And turn aside the poor in the gate" (Amos 5:12). This led God to reject the worship of His people. There was absolutely no awareness of a life of sacrifice, which was central to having an authentic relationship with God. So Leviticus and Amos aren't contradictory but complementary.

Leviticus shows us that justice and compassion are central to worship, and Amos shows the consequence when justice and compassion, which are the weightier matters of a consecrated life, are ignored. Jesus sheds light on this principle in Luke 11:42. "But Woe to you Pharisees! For you pay tithe of mint and rue and every kind of garden herb, and yet disregard justice and the love of God; but these are the things you should have done without neglecting the others."

Evident in the book of Leviticus was that God wanted the people to live a consecrated life. They had followed God out of Egypt into the Promised Land. Their calling was to be a nation that was different from the nations around them. Their history portrays a nation that adopted many of the customs of the surrounding pagan nations, especially when it came to worship. They came to see worship as a performance to put on in front of God. Worse, it seems they used worship to excuse an unrighteous life. Christ brought a renewed perspective of worship, one that focused not on any religious symbolism but on worship in spirit and truth, a phrase first uttered by Jesus Christ as a fulfillment of the Law. Jesus said, "But an hour is coming, and now is, when the true worshipers will worship the Father in spirit and truth, for such people the Father seeks to be His worshipers" (John 4:23).

So at its very heart, worship was always intended to be an offering. The shortcoming in our thinking, however, is to limit worship to the events of an organized worship experience in a structure built for religious gatherings. In the elaborate sacrificial system, feasts and special worship gatherings known as solemn assemblies were corporate worship experiences that were a celebration of living with the one true God. This celebration consisted of renewing the covenant of living with God and practicing His ethics and love.

In other words, corporate worship is celebrating and offering an already changed life, one lived in consecrated devotion to Yahweh. This is why the prophet Amos admonished the people for not practicing justice. Entering into a covenant of salvation with God is evidenced by a life aligning itself with the same compassion as God—a holy life. God has always expected a life set apart from those who worship Him because worship is a response to the presence of God in our lives.

The Living Temple

Worship is a misunderstood practice in almost every culture and every religion, including Christianity. We spend so much energy trying to set the atmosphere for worship, follow the plan for worship, or conjure up the presence of God that we miss the essence of worship. Worship is a response to the continual presence of God in our lives; it is not trying to usher in the presence of God through meditation, or through fanciful, stately, classical, or modern expressions of music.

Christians view the facilities where we gather for worship much like other religions view a temple. A temple is a place of worship, so we think of the sanctuaries of our church buildings as the place of worship for Christians. This is dangerously incomplete. If the only occasion we express worship is on Sunday morning when we fill our churches, then our relationship with God is like our sanctuaries on Monday through Saturday: empty.

The Christian faith speaks of a different kind of temple. Our temple is not made of stones and elaborate decorations; it is made of flesh and blood. In 1 Corinthians 6:18–19, Paul states, "Flee immorality. Every other sin that a man commits is outside the body, but the immoral man sins against his own body. Or do you not know that your body is a Temple of the Holy Spirit who is in you, whom you have from God, and that you are not your own?" When we commit to follow Jesus, our bodies become the temples of God, the residences of God and are places of worship.

It is evident in 1 Corinthians 6:18, when Paul says to flee immorality, that the actions we take with our bodies are consequential. Our bodies are sacred places. Our bodies are not just occasional temples, part-time temples, or "only when it is convenient for me" temples. They are the full-time expression of the eternal God, making Himself known in and through us. See, the temple of the church walks around. It's not a physical location anymore. It's in us, and it is us—both individually and collectively.

The Temple in Jerusalem was also a place for a specific kind of worship—the offering of sacrifices. That we are meant to be living sacrifices speaks to God's intention and plan for us to not only be a place where God resides but an instrument of worship to God. Our bodies, these vessels of worship, are the visible symbol of God's presence in the world. They are to be living sacrifices, giving testimony to the work of transformation that God is doing in our lives and in the world.

Seeing and experiencing our bodies as the Temple of the Holy Spirit puts our lives in the context of being immersed in the presence of God, not pursuing His presence by creating the right mood and music for worship. God's power is at work through us, each and every day, as we live with Him.

We are not smartphones, entering into a "time" of worship to get charged up for the week ahead and slowly running out of power as the week progresses, until the next worship service when we are connected to God by professional worship leaders. Believers are wed to God, constantly connected to Him through the Holy Spirit. We are the children of God, His prized creations, involved in continuous worship through our consecrated lives. This changes the goal of gathered worship. Gathered worship is a continuation of the life of worship lived out the previous week in the workplace, classroom, civic involvement, and family, not merely a place to receive inspiration for the week to come. Our entire existence is to be offered as worship.

The question, "Is my life offered as worship?" has caused a sea change of thinking for me over the past several years, related to faith in Jesus Christ. In Malachi 2:13–17, the prophet says that God rejects the worship—or the singing, dancing, and music associated with worship in a religious gathering—because the men had divorced the wives of their youth with no cause. Their wives had not committed adultery, the men just wanted another wife. So authentic worship in a religious gathering, such as a church service, has always been an outpouring of our character.

The truly authentic encounter with God is the offering of worship that we give daily, evidenced by who we are—the way we live. The person who doesn't live the daily offering of worship will never move beyond short-lived worship thrills or the sentimental thoughts of childhood church experiences, and—most tragically—will never experience the abundant life. We will never know the joy of being free in Christ where our lives are an authentic expression of our inward being. Worship will be just an exercise in excitement, trying to get God's attention or possibly searching for that worship experience that makes us feel better. We will forever be trapped in worship as a transaction with God. Worship was never intended to be a transaction with God but a transformative process.

CHAPTER 3

TRANSACTIONAL VERSUS TRANSFORMATIONAL WORSHIP

Transactions are ingrained in our lives. We pay money for particular services or products, make business deals with detailed understandings, and exchange handshakes on verbal agreements. This is such a prominent part of our culture that it is difficult, if not impossible, to think of our lives as anything more than a series of transactions. Want a gallon of milk? Pay a certain amount of money. Want an automobile? Either pay the cash, or take out a loan and pay the full amount over an agreed number of months. Business dealings are the accepted societal norm for how we conduct our lives. No one is offended by these types of financial agreements. In reality, we become suspicious of anything that doesn't have an understood transaction. If something is "free," we automatically conclude that there is a catch or gimmick.

Many friendships are built on common transactions as well. Some people desire the companionship of certain people in their peer groups so much that they always pay for lunch, coffee, or a greens fee. It gives control to the person who pays but inhibits true joy, as the person who always picks up the tab never gets to experience the confidence that the other person accepts him for who he is, not merely for what he can provide.

When it comes to our dearest relationships, however, overt transactions offend us. A husband who withholds affection from his wife unless he gets his way in a decision or who only gives affection when he wants sex is seen as a manipulator or jerk. A wife who withholds sex unless her husband helps with the housework, takes her to a nice restaurant, or treats her to a manicure is seen as high maintenance and manipulative. Attempted manipulations are commonplace between some husbands and wives but are not restricted to marriage.

In our relationship with God, this transactional mind-set permeates our thinking and actions. We catch ourselves making deals with God. "God, I'll go to church for the rest of my life if you will just get me out of this foxhole alive." Or, consciously or subconsciously, we take our children to church because we somehow think it obligates God to make sure they become respected and respectable people. There really is no limit to the transactional aspect of our faith, as commonly understood, but this common practice of how we relate to and bargain with God is destructive. It destroys the communal nature of a faith relationship between the Creator God and His creation: us.

The best marriages do not keep scorecards of the bargains or agreements we make with our spouses. The best is realized when husbands and wives cherish one another. This cherishing is demonstrated in the love they give one another, not by keeping track of what has or has not been given and then measuring out a portion of affection and devotion commensurate with what each one has received. It is the same with God. What He prizes above everything is a person's heart—a person's heartfelt affection and will. God desires to be cherished.

On the face of it, Deuteronomy 6:1–9 seems to be one big transaction. Deuteronomy 6:3 states, "O Israel, you should listen and be careful to do it, that it may be well with you and that you may multiply greatly, just as the Lord, the God of your fathers, has promised you, in a land flowing with milk and honey." We may conclude that things will go well for us if we teach, change our personal behavior, and proclaim to the world around us that we love God (Deuteronomy 6:7–9). What we overlook in many instances is that God is not proposing a transaction but a transformed heart. "These words, which I am commanding you today shall be on your heart" (Deuteronomy 6:6). A changed heart is the beginning point in a life of worship. This transformation sets "living in promise" in motion. Our actions that bring about life to the full must come from humble hearts full of worship. It is impossible to overstate how essential our love for God is to our spiritual existence and sustenance. When this transformation begins in our hearts, we begin the transition—from being identified by the events, morals, culture, and expectations of the world around us to being identified as children of God.

Identity is important. It gives meaning to who we are. William, my son, played four-year-old T-ball. When registration opened for five-year-old T-ball the next year, I asked him if he wanted to play T-ball again. He said, "Dad, I'm not a T-ball player; I'm a baseball player." I immediately signed him up to play baseball with the six-year-olds. He longed to be a baseball player, and he wanted to be identified as one as soon as possible. We must find our identity in Jesus Christ. We long to be identified as His follower as soon as possible. This ushers in a realignment in our lives. No longer are we drawn to live according to the world, but we are at complete peace to live in the riches of God's expectations. The expectations are not a series of restrictive rules but the proactive offering of our lives in true worship.

Refocused Worship

One of the key perspectives that Christ had to refocus was His disciples' perspective of worship. Their faith was centered on worship of the true God. The Temple was the center of worship for the Israelites in Jesus's day. Place and conformity were of utmost importance, especially for the religious leaders.

Many times, we look back on this preoccupation the Israelites had with place and structure and respond with judgment because of how it was distorted and abused by the Pharisees and Sadducees. We forget that for many common people, including Mary and Joseph, the parents of Jesus, the Temple was a central part of a truly heartfelt and authentic faith. This was a heritage shared by thousands of God's chosen of that day.

Worship in the Jewish faith was to be an expression that went beyond the customs of the Temple and the annual festivals. This was Jesus's conclusion when He had His encounter with the woman at the well. Jesus had a private conversation with this Samaritan woman, which broke many customs of that day. This conversation could have been absorbed into oblivion, but Jesus told His disciples what He had discussed with the woman because there was a vital perspective of spirituality in the encounter that couldn't be overlooked—a perspective that would change the lives of the disciples. By stating, "There is coming a day when you will worship in spirit and truth" (John 4:23), Jesus wanted these men, who would establish and build His church, to understand that worship in the New Covenant would be expressed by transformational worship from the heart—worship that takes place in the context of our relationships with God and others.

Worship through Romance and Commitment

Revelation 19:7–9 and 21:9 refer to the church as the bride of Christ. It's completely within the framework of Scripture to compare our relationships with God to that between a husband and wife. There are two essential traits in a successful marriage. One is romance, and the other is commitment. Early in marriage, most couples are much more energized by romance rather than commitment. It's a lot more fun, going out to dinner and spending intimate time together, than just having the day-in, day-out commitment of being a devoted spouse and parent. Tending to this commitment is the difficult work of marriage. It's much easier to look forward to the romance, but a maturing relationship begins to find fulfillment in the day-to-day commitment of marriage, without neglecting the romance.

Our culture emphasizes romance in our relationships with our girlfriend or boyfriend, fiancé or fiancée, and spouse. We see this in television shows and movies. This emphasis is transferred to our relationship with God, especially as it relates to worship. Our relationship with God should involve aspects of commitment and romance. In fact, our romance—with our spouse and with God—is only acceptable and meaningful if it is backed up by commitment and sealed in unshakable loyalty and sacrifice.

It may seem odd to talk about parts of our relationship with God by using the term *romance*, but in essence, many parts of gathered worship are similar to romance. Our songs, hymns, and prayers verbally express our love to God and what He means to us. This is analogous to what we do when we relate to our spouses. My romance of Sheri, my wife, is expressed by affirmations of my love for her. Occasionally, I sing to her, and sometimes I write to her. Similarly, the songs and hymns we sing to God are verbal expressions of love, but it is only true worship if it is backed up by our commitment, just as true romance of one's spouse is backed up by commitment.

A marriage that is built only on romance is a relationship in danger. A marriage that is built on just commitment is dull and robotic and also in danger. In the same way, a relationship with God that is built on only the romance of corporate worship is a relationship in danger. Think how your spouse would feel if the only time she or he knew of your love was on Friday nights. It could include dinner, a movie, and spectacular physical intimacy, but there would not be any other time during the week that you thought of your spouse or the relationship you said was so meaningful and important to you. How long do you think the vitality in that relationship would last? Your spouse would start to see you for what you are: a person who is concerned only with what you need from the relationship. Romance alone cannot carry the freight in a relationship. Marriage must be carried by commitment and romance combined. Romance must be a part of the expression of the commitment that is already there.

Almost everyone who has dated has experienced heartbreak and pain when someone's words were incongruent with his or her actions. A person may say he or she loves someone, but it becomes evident that the words are only uttered because they are expected or because of something wanted in the relationship. God may see that same kind of trait when a church is gathered for worship. We gather on Sunday morning and tell Him how much we love and care for Him, thank Him for His blessings, and tell Him how wonderful He is and how much we adore Him. The next morning, however, we may have a completely different mind-set, thinking that all we do on Monday through Saturday has no bearing on what we said on Sunday. For many, this experience of worship plays out weekly. It grieves God when we say all the right things but never validate our words by our actions. When we grasp the seriousness with which God expects worship to take place in every aspect of our lives, we will understand true worship. This is the beginning of worshiping in spirit and truth.

That's what God was trying to teach the leaders of the nation of Israel. They were saying all the right things during organized worship (romance) but were not basing it on the truly important aspects of daily worship (commitment). They neglected the kind of worship expected by God—caring for the orphan and widow, justice, and commitment to their marriages. They did not deal justly with people. The judges took bribes. There was no justice in their land. Their lives were marked by their lack of commitment and their perversion of worship.

Commitment is the engine for lasting romance in our marriages and in our worship. The commitment must be present first for the romance to bloom fully. Modern-day Christians must give attention to our commitment to God, Monday through Saturday, so that the romance offered on Sundays is accepted by God and can find full expression and full blossom in our churches and in our lives. That's what God expects from us. This is "our spiritual service of worship," just as Paul states in Romans 12:1. It does not bog us down; it frees us. It's something that's reasonable and attainable, just as in a marriage relationship, it's reasonable for a husband and wife to keep the vows they made to one another. It's also reasonable for God to expect us to keep the promises we make in gathered worship on Sundays.

Life-altering behavior requires a foundation. Without a foundation, we fall into the trap of designing lives of our choosing—building a life on shaky theological ground. This concept of worship should not give us the idea that we can live any way we wish and call it worship. We must construct a proper foundation for a life of worship, and the first part of this foundation is understanding who we worship.

PART 2

WHO WE WORSHIP

CHAPTER 4

THE LIVING GOD

We worship the living God—the God who intersects the world. He has revealed Himself as the living God throughout Scripture. He interacted with Adam and Eve in a personal way in the Garden of Eden by giving them instructions and meeting them in the evening. God's covenant with Abram entailed showing him the land he was going to possess (Genesis 12:1). Moses encountered the living God at the burning bush when God revealed His name to Moses: "I am who I am" (Exodus 3:14). God reveals Himself as the present God. The repetition of *I am* indicates God is intentionally and dynamically present with us—His children.[2] God continued His interaction with the nation of Israel through prophets, kings, and finally through Jesus Christ—His full and final revelation. God desires to be known as the living God by the entire world so He became flesh and lived among men (John 1:14). God did all of this because He is holy.

---

[2] Walter C. Kaiser, "Exodus", *The Expositor's Bible Commentary* (Grand Rapids, MI: Zondervan, 1990), 2:321.

The Holy God

God is holy. Isaiah 6 gives a powerful description of God's infinite wonder and marvelous mercy. Angels surround Him, singing His praises. "Holy, Holy, Holy, is the Lord of hosts, The whole earth is full of His glory" (Isaiah 6:3). Holy means "set apart." Christians often have trouble explaining the majesty and wonder of God. God is transcendent, which means God is wholly other than His creation, but we only know His transcendence and holiness because of His immanence; that is, His purposeful choice to be present and interact with the humans He created. When we speak of His holiness, we should only speak to what has been revealed in Scripture. To ascribe anything to His holiness other than what has been revealed is merely speculation and quite probably idolatrous ruminations.

This description—"I saw the Lord sitting on a throne, lofty and exalted, with the train of His robe filling the temple"—found in Isaiah 6:1 is among many revelations of His holiness. We also see His holiness recorded in Exodus 3:2–6. When God encountered Moses in the burning bush, He instructed Moses to take his sandals off because Moses was standing on holy ground.

Both descriptions, in Isaiah and Exodus, reveal God's heart filled with love for, and deliverance of people, which expresses His holiness. The Isaiah 6 and Exodus 3 passages, while powerful and full of splendor, lead us to embrace the majestic expression of His holiness, which is His mercy, evidenced by God calling and sending Isaiah and Moses. God is indeed transcendent, but His holiness is tangible—revealed through His immanence. Recognizing and celebrating God's holiness is essential, but embracing and expressing His mercy is how we align ourselves with His holiness and become set apart. We are not God and are not perfect, but we are called to be holy as He is holy (1 Peter 1:16; cf. Leviticus 11:44).

God's holiness is not hidden but is something that we can model in order to practice righteousness. Descriptions of God's holiness that keep God unknowable and untouchable run amiss of the purpose of God's self-revelation and holiness. There is a perilous safety in creating a God who is indescribable and unknowable because it relieves us of the requirement of being touched by Him and—more important—being aligned with Him.

The testimony of Scripture is that God was touchable in the person of Jesus Christ. 1 John 1:1 states, "What was from the beginning, what we have heard, what we have seen with our eyes, what we have looked at and touched with our hands, concerning the Word of Life." He is knowable by anyone who chooses to be touched by the proclamation of truth found in Jesus Christ and placing faith in Him, thereby joining the divine fellowship (1 John 1:1–3). In God's sovereignty, He chose to be known.

The Sovereign God

God is sovereign. He has complete authority over everything and has the freedom to act as He chooses, which He does. At least three prevalent concepts of sovereignty influence our thinking. First, in the context of a nation, we think of its ability to govern itself and be self-determining. Second, those who do not acknowledge or believe in God may see themselves as self-governing or self-determining or that their lives are determined by fate or chance. The third concept is that God is sovereign over the world and its events.

The concept of God's sovereignty has been influenced by the machine age and the subsequent technology age. The advent of the machine age brought precision to manufacturing that has only become more precise with the invention and development of the microprocessor and modern technology. Because of the precision that surrounds our lives, our concept of sovereignty, as it relates to God, is impacted. We assign God's sovereignty the same traits as are evident in a machine or the latest technology, controlling every tiny movement of our lives. God indeed has the authority and ability to control every aspect of the universe and everything in our lives. He has chosen to relate to us, however, in His sovereignty based in the context of Scripture.

In relation to Scripture, the word sovereignty is used in the context of a monarch or king. If you live in the realm of a king, he has authority over you, but you have a choice in how you relate to him. You can be a loyal subject who works for the same purposes as the king. You can be an appreciative subject, recognizing the benefits of living in the kingdom but only doing what is required to make you and your family safe and comfortable without being concerned with sacrificing anything. You can relate as an indifferent subject, not caring who is in charge. Or you can relate to the king in open rebellion, attempting to thwart his work and purposes. All subjects, however, no matter how they choose to relate to the king, are under the king's sovereignty.

We too have the same choice in relationship with God. We can relate to God as loyal, appreciative, indifferent, or rebellious subjects. 2 Peter 3:9 states, "The Lord is not slow about His promise, as some count slowness, but is patient toward you, not wishing for any to perish but for all to come to repentance." God desires all people to be loyal subjects, but the testimony of God's sovereignty is this: He has chosen not to intervene in every individual situation and decision. However, no matter how we, as individuals or nations, choose to relate to Him, He controls the ultimate outcome of events.

He longs for all people to come to salvation, but in other words, our choices to rebel against God do not deter His work. "God causes all things to work together for good to those who love God, to those who are called according to His purpose" (Romans 8:28). This doesn't mean that everything that happens is good, but that He works all things together for redemption. God's sovereignty means that anyone desiring to be a loyal subject of God, the King of the universe, is not left in abandonment. God sends people—you and me—to show them and to proclaim to them that Jesus is the way, the only way for entry into the kingdom of God, so they will become loyal subjects also.

God, in His sovereignty, desires the world to know Him and His love for humanity. He has chosen and predestined His loyal subjects to bring the message of Jesus to the people of this world, including the appreciative subjects, the indifferent subjects, and the rebellious subjects. He is calling the appreciative subjects to embrace a bigger vision of the world and their role in it. He invites the indifferent subjects to understand how important God is, how worthy He is of their lives. He works through the Holy Spirit to bring the rebellious subjects to repentance and faith.

So much of our theology attempts to take all the mystery out of our relationships with God. Our desire to have everything explained to us becomes paramount. It also leads us to feel the need to have answers as we witness and proclaim the gospel and give testimony to a relationship with God. We latch onto the theological concepts that bring us the most security and comfort. If we are honest with ourselves, God has never worked exclusively inside any of our theological explanations.

In the New Covenant, He encounters the entire world, Jew and Gentile with the declaration of being present with us in Jesus, who is called Immanuel—"God with us." Now, all people have the choice to believe. Some will believe in Jesus as Savior, and some will not (John 3:16). When people come to believe in Jesus they are called to a primary task, which is to be a blessing to all people through God's love, as realized in the life, death, and resurrection of Jesus Christ. We are to do good works in Christ Jesus that God prepared in advance for us to do (Ephesians 2:10). The first step to fulfilling the call and purpose that God has for us is to understand and accept who Jesus is—the full and final revelation of God—the Christ.

CHAPTER 5

THE CHRIST

A common weakness of many Christians, especially in the initial stages of faith, is a stunningly shallow understanding of who Christ is. This is not unique to this century or the modern church, nor is it the exclusive domain of any age group. Many know basic facts about Jesus, that He is the Son of God, our Savior, and He brings salvation. Some actively believe and can share what Jesus did. What is missing is an understanding of Jesus as a transformer of peoples' lives, not just the Savior who forgives our sins. Jesus not only saves us *from* our old lives but saves us *to* the new, transformed lives that we can realize only when we allow our understanding of who He is to work in us.

To do this, it is imperative that Christians understand the person and work of Jesus so we can live our life to the full potential of what He wants. Jesus, along with others in the Bible, make statements that paint a clear picture of who He is. Others' statements concerning Jesus, as well as Jesus's own "I am" statements recorded by the apostle John, will be presented. First, others' statements about Jesus.

The Word

"In the beginning was the Word, and the Word was with God, and the Word was God" (John 1:1).

John describes Jesus as the "Word," which is translated from the Greek word *logos*, meaning "divine presence." John's important testimony is that Jesus is the divine presence and that He is eternal. Jesus has been in eternal relationship with God, and He is God. Everything Scripture reveals about God applies to Jesus because they are one. The first chapter of John says that everything was created through the Word (John 1:3). Therefore, in Jesus Christ we find the full revelation of God, the one who put a human face and human existence on the eternal, living, holy, and sovereign God. John says, "And the Word became flesh, and dwelt among us" (John 1:14). Now the eternal God, Yahweh, always understood as the living God, could be touched and seen. He is Immanuel.

Immanuel, God with Us

"'Behold, the virgin shall be with child and shall bear a Son, and they shall call His name Immanuel', which translated means, 'God with us'" (Matthew 1:23).

Scripture testifies that God is living and guides and directs His children. In Jesus, God is personal and physical—He became human to live among men and women. Today, Jesus is present with us through every victory, every defeat, every accomplishment, every failure, and every good act. Jesus is with us, not merely as an observer of what we do; He is active in what we do. We can't hold Him at arm's length when we place our faith in Him. He embraces us, and we embrace Him in the fullness of life, in all of life. This embrace is everlasting, and through this embrace, we experience the life to which He has called each of us—the life of sacrifice that He modeled.

He is not a god confined to a memorial we construct in our homes or only visit on prescribed days of religious devotion and observance. He is "with us" in the journey—a journey fraught with challenges and danger. But we do not fear the journey or fret about the outcome because we rest in the security that He will never forsake or abandon us. He is our companion in life and a continual participant in our lives of worship. God pursued us through Jesus. We trust that Jesus is in us, and we are in Him as we live each day. He is Immanuel—God with us, forever. He became God with us so we could know Him as Christ, the Son of God.

The Son of the Living God

"You are the Christ, the Son of the Living God" (Matthew 16:16).

Peter uttered his deepest insight into who Jesus was when he made this declaration. It is the most foundational of all the statements of who Jesus is. These few words are packed full of theological implications. From the meaning of these few words, we can understand the purpose and identity of Christ. It was this revelation upon which Jesus would build His church; it was the bedrock of doctrinal explanations of who Jesus asserted himself to be.

First, *Christ* is from a Greek word meaning "the anointed one of God" and is equivalent to the Hebrew word *Messiah*. Throughout the Bible, anointing signifies that the person who is anointed has a special role to perform, a role sanctioned by God. Anointing was performed by pouring oil on a person who was set apart for a special role. For example, Samuel anointed David as the next king of Israel (1 Samuel 16:12–13). All priests were anointed (Exodus 30:30). The anointing did not occur because of human intentions and desires but because of God's instruction. God is the one who anoints, through someone whom He instructs to do so on His behalf.

Two passages in the Gospels refer to Jesus's anointing. When Jesus taught in the synagogue, after being tempted in the desert by

Satan, He read from the prophet Isaiah. "The Spirit of the Lord is upon Me, Because He anointed Me to preach the gospel to the poor. He has sent Me to proclaim release to the captives, And recovery of sight to the blind, To set free those who are oppressed, To proclaim the favorable year of the Lord" (Luke 4:18–19). Jesus went on to say that this Scripture had been fulfilled in their hearing.

In Mark 14:1–11, Jesus is anointed when Mary pours oil on His head. When she is reprimanded by those in attendance, Jesus replies, "She has done what she could; she has anointed My body beforehand for the burial" (Mark 14:8). Therefore, Christ's role and purpose on earth was ordained by God—planned by God. Jesus was anointed by the Holy Spirit to bring the message of hope through His life. He was anointed by His chosen servant, Mary, just prior to His crucifixion to prepare Jesus for the Cross.[3] God ordained Jesus to fulfill the purpose for which He was sent by God.

Second, "Son of the living God" signifies that Jesus has the same character as the Heavenly Father. In Hebrew thinking, a son not only inherited the physical characteristics of his father but also his character. We have a similar old saying: "The apple doesn't fall far from the tree." While an ordinary son would not carry all the physical and spiritual characteristics of his father, it was different with Jesus, regarding spiritual traits. "For in Him all the fullness of Deity dwells in bodily form" (Colossians 2:9).

Third, attaching the phrase "living God" left people no doubt with whom Jesus was identifying. Only Yahweh is described as being the living God. As mentioned earlier, Yahweh is translated as "I Am who I Am." This intentional and dynamic presence was realized through the deliverance of God's people from Egypt. Jesus's intentional and dynamic presence is realized through His work to deliver us from sin.

---

[3] The woman's name is revealed as Mary in the parallel passage found in John 12:1–8.

Behold the Lamb

"Behold, the Lamb of God who takes away the sin of the world!" (John 1:29).

This proclamation is rich in meaning. John the Baptist was "preaching a baptism of repentance for the forgiveness of sins" (Mark 1:4). But Jesus's ministry and work completely dwarfed the ministry of John the Baptist because John's ministry was limited by geography and physical presence. The ministry of Jesus is for the entire world. This is possible because Jesus is the Lamb of God.

In addition to the annual sacrifice of atonement made by the high priest there were the daily sacrifices of two lambs, one each morning and one each evening (Exodus 29:39). As mentioned previously, this was to be a continual sacrifice throughout all future generations. John proclaimed that now Jesus is that continual, eternal sacrifice for the entire world. There is no need to offer another sacrifice for the sins we have committed, intentionally or unintentionally; that work has been completed in Jesus Christ (Hebrews 10:1–18). His death is the means through which God makes clear His original intentions of salvation offered to the entire human race, regardless of whether a person is a genetic descendent of Abraham or not. Jesus's sacrifice testifies that He is our salvation.

Jesus

"She will bear a Son; and you shall call His name Jesus, for He will save His people from their sins" (Matthew 1:21).

The name *Jesus* is derived from the Hebrew name Joshua or *Yeshua*, which means "Yahweh saves or Yahweh brings salvation." The purpose and ministry of Jesus was seen before the outset of His earthly life. His name signified Joseph and Mary's awareness that the events leading up to Jesus's birth were a harbinger of greater things to come. They were told to name Him Jesus, so they did.

Herod feared a rival king, which is the reason he sought to have Jesus killed. But the role of Jesus was unbelievably superior to Herod's concerns. Jesus was not going to rule territories of land but the territories comprised of the hearts of men and women, calling them to the living water of salvation. He was sent to earth to bring about a permanent kingdom, not merely one ruled by men. He was the child of promise—the Messiah. This title, "Messiah," is a title Jesus claimed for Himself as well and begins the series of "I am" statements found in the gospel of John.

I Am Messiah

"The woman said to Him, 'I know that Messiah is coming (He who is called Christ); when that One comes, He will declare all things to us.' Jesus said to her, 'I who speak to you am He'" (John 4:25–26).

Messiah means "anointed one." Jesus's first claim about His identity is that He is the Anointed One from God, the one who fulfills the promise of salvation and deliverance of God's people. The people of first-century Palestine desired and believed that the Messiah would come to deliver them from the grip of the Roman Empire and usher in a better life. It was common for people to claim to be the Messiah. So the people would listen to a man who made that claim, but they remained skeptical until it was proven.

This "I am" statement is obscured a little because of how it is translated. However, *Ego eimi* are the same two Greek words found in the subsequent "I am" statements in the gospel of John. For ease of reading, the "I" and the "am" are separated by the clarifying words "who speak to you" in the English translation. *Ego* is a pronoun translated as "I," and *eimi* is a verb translated as "I am." So in each of the "I am" statements made by Jesus, He is actually saying "I, I am." The repetition of the personal pronoun "I" is an emphatic way of saying "I, and no one else, am."[4]

The incredible aspect of Jesus's self-revelation, in which He claimed to be the Messiah, is in *where* He first made the claim and *to whom* He made that claim. The Messiah was expected to set up His kingdom and rule from Jerusalem, presumably to the self-defined rightful heirs of promise. Instead, Jesus revealed His identity in Samaria, to a Samaritan adulteress. This may seem unimportant, but it is an immediate example of the claim Jesus made to Nicodemus in John 3:16—that God loves the entire world and sent His Son to bring salvation to everyone who believes. The Samaritans were despised by the Israelites. Many Jews would walk around the region of Samaria to avoid contact with them.

In addition Jesus's first revelation of Himself as the Messiah was to a woman with no respect in the town. The fact that He went to a woman revealed that women would have the same access to salvation that men had. No longer would they be identified merely by who they gave birth to or who they were married to. Now it was clear they would be held accountable to the same standard as the men regarding the decision they would make concerning God's Son.

Finally, the woman was a social outcast because of her actions, indicated by coming to the well at midday, alone. By the prevailing religious standards of the day she was doomed to strike out: wrong race, wrong gender, and wrong behavior. Jesus could have gone to the religious establishment to gain their approval for His ministry, but He demonstrated through His actions that His salvation was for all people. He recognized that the only validation He needed was to fulfill the will of God. That is the only validation we should desire as well.

The disciples missed the conversation between Jesus and the Samaritan woman because they had gone into the city to buy food

---

[4] Herschel H. Hobbs, *An Exposition of the Gospel of John* (Grand Rapids, MI: Baker Book House, 1968), 104.

for lunch. Jesus confuses them by saying He has food to eat that they don't know about and that food is to do the will of God and accomplish His work (John 4:32–34). Jesus essentially states that His nourishment and sustenance come from fulfilling God's will for His life. In this, He finds His purpose and spiritual nutrition. This spiritual food is His life—the life He offers to us.

I Am the Bread of Life

"I am the bread of life; he who comes to Me will not hunger, and he who believes in Me will never thirst" (John 6:35).

The context of Jesus's self-declaration is an extension of the first "I am" statement. Just the day before this statement was spoken, Jesus performed the miracle of feeding over five thousand people with five barley loaves and two fish. The people He fed came back to Jesus so that they could receive another free meal. The people Jesus encountered held a common belief that the Messiah would usher in an era of abundance and plenty, supernaturally provided by God, based on Israel's deliverance from Egypt by Moses. When Moses delivered the children of Israel out of Egypt, God provided manna for them while they were in the wilderness.

The people expected the Messiah to provide daily food. When Jesus referred to himself as the One sent from heaven, the people immediately asked for a sign to give proof of His claim. They saw Jesus as someone who could possibly meet their physical needs. Jesus wanted the crowd to get their focus off temporal and ordinary things. He needed them to focus on something permanent that lasts for eternity. He desired them to recognize the deeper need only He could fill. Jesus did not come to be merely the provider of our daily bread but to be our Bread of Life. Daily bread only fills us temporarily, but the Bread of Life fills us permanently. Just as ordinary food becomes a part of who we are, Jesus, as the sacrificed Bread of Life, becomes a part of who we are.

At the Last Supper, just before He went to the Cross, Jesus invited the disciples, His dearest friends, to partake in symbolically eating His flesh and drinking His blood through the bread and wine served during Passover. His reference to eating His flesh and drinking His blood may seem gross and offensive to us, but the symbols are deliberately challenging.

Jesus Christ desires that the sacrifice He modeled to the world on the Cross become a part of who we are. Just as Jesus said His food was to do the will of His Father, our food is the sacrifice of Jesus (John 4:24). His nourishment and sustenance was to do the Father's will. Our nourishment and sustenance is to be transformed and identified with His sacrifice and to live His sacrifice. This is communion with Christ.

Many Christians never reach a state in their lives where we are content, find joy, and cease to long for something more fulfilling in life because we have never eaten the bread or drunk the wine of sacrifice. We consume the elements of communion, but never let Jesus's sacrifice transform us into a living sacrifice and become a part of who we are—our identities. The assimilation of His sacrifice into our very being is when we are forever cured from spiritual hunger and thirst. We become satisfied with Jesus because He provides never-ending spiritual nourishment. Jesus draws us to this never-ending nourishment of our spirit because He is the Light of the World.

I Am the Light of the World

"I am the Light of the world; he who follows Me will not walk in the darkness, but will have the Light of life" (John 8:12).

Many people, even those who do good things, never experience Jesus as the Light of the world because they never believe in Him. They settle for just seeing natural things at work in their lives and in the lives of others. They do good things through committed service, such as feeding the poor, housing the homeless, and caring for orphans, all of which meet real needs. The services they provide are crucial and beneficial for those who receive them. These people rob themselves, however, of seeing any supernatural work through their good deeds because they perform them entirely by their own strength with just material and physical resources. Jesus is the means for us to meet the physical *and* spiritual needs of others with supernatural power. This is the Light of life. We possess the Light of life when we come to recognize and embrace Jesus as the Light of the world.

Jesus claimed to be the Light during the Feast of Tabernacles, also called the Feast of Booths, one of three festivals every Israelite was commanded in the Law to observe. It was observed by lighting candles in the Temple in Jerusalem. The lights were extinguished after the feast concluded. In this context, Jesus says that He is the Light of the world. In John 8, we find that Jesus had been teaching in the Temple during the entire seven-day feast. On the last day, His teaching generated various responses in the crowd among the Pharisees and the chief priests. Some in the crowd believed in Him (John 8:30), some accused Him of having a demon (John 8:48), and some tried to kill Him (John 8:59). The proclamation of who Jesus is has always elicited different reactions, revealing the hearts of men and women.

Christ's claim to be the Light of the world was more than a metaphor. It was a means by which believers came into a relationship with God that Christ envisioned and desired. God desires His children to be certain of His plan and purpose for their lives, beginning with forgiveness of sin, but encompassing much more. Jesus shined significance into the Feast of Booths. The lights that would be extinguished at the end of the festival and then relit the next year could be replaced by the Light of Jesus that would dwell in them, a life-giving Light that will never be put out.

Before Jesus finished teaching that day, they heard His claim that God sent Him, and that He was from above (John 8:16, 23). Jesus taught that unless they believe they will die in their sins (John

8:24). Jesus told them the crucifixion will confirm and reveal who He is (John 8:28). The people heard that those who continue in the teaching of Jesus will know the truth, and the truth will set them free (John 8:31–32), and those that seek to destroy Jesus and His work are in spiritual alignment with Satan (John 8:44). These are bold statements, but not nearly as bold as when Jesus concluded this interaction by stating the fourth "I am" statement which spoke to His eternal nature and authority.

Before Abraham Was Born I Am

"Truly, truly, I say to you, before Abraham was born, I am" (John 8:58).

Jesus's fourth and most bold "I am" statement nearly incited a riot. When Jesus spoke the words "before Abraham was I am," the people picked up stones to throw at Him because they knew the significance of His claim (John 8:59). Jesus's incredible statement claimed that His existence predated God's covenant with Abraham, equating Himself to God. The religious leaders of the first century, much like some today, sought exclusivity and special consideration with salvation because of ancestral ties and who they knew. These leaders of Jesus's day falsely taught that only the genetic descendants of Abraham had a chance at a relationship with God even though there were gentile converts to Judaism in ancient Israel (Exodus 12:48-49; Isaiah 56:6-7). In reality, they, like anyone who claims a special relationship with God based on human relationship or ancestry, had a spiritual kinship with evil—Satan.

Jesus claimed to be with God since the beginning. This truth would force the religious leaders to abandon one of their most dearly held cultural and religious beliefs—that God was restricted to work through the descendants of Abraham because of the covenant God made with them. By claiming to predate Abraham, Jesus made an overt statement that He is eternal with God. Therefore, the genetic descendants of Abraham were never the doorkeepers of salvation, nor were they the only recipients of salvation. They were to lead others to the threshold of the door, just as we are to do, but we never proclaim anything other than Jesus as the door.

I Am the Door

"I am the door; if anyone enters through Me, he will be saved, and will go in and out and find pasture" (John 10:9).

In ancient Israel, shepherds would take their sheep each morning to a nearby valley and lead them to green grass and water. Several flocks grazed in the fields together, even though they had different shepherds. Toward the end of the day, each shepherd would call his sheep together and then lead them to a cave or a structure to find shelter for the night. The door was the entryway to safety. Jesus uses this common cultural understanding of the day to illustrate who He is. In this simple analogy, Jesus claims to be the Savior. Those who enter the door through Him will be saved.

It is explicitly clear in John 10:1–5 that some will try to enter the fellowship another way, but Jesus states unequivocally that these people are dangerous—thieves and robbers. In this distinction between those who enter salvation through Jesus Christ and those who try to enter by another means, we discover an important truth. Everyone must enter into salvation through Jesus to find full spiritual affinity with God.

Those who try to enter the fellowship without Jesus will rob, kill, and destroy the spiritual lives of believers. Before knowing Jesus, we seek our own self-interest or demand to live by our own power. When we live without Jesus, we attempt to arrange our world to provide for our own security. The unavoidable result of living in this self-interest is constructing our own values.

Religion that is built on our own values becomes artificial and without life, seeking to exert itself through natural and worldly means. The reason we must come into the flock through Jesus is that He transforms us from the thieves and robbers of others' spiritual vitality into people who seek not our own will and fulfillment but God's will, channeling our entire lives through worship of Him. By coming into fellowship through Jesus as the door into God's kingdom, we give witness to our humility that our characters and personalities can only be transformed through Him. Our goal as Christians is to get people involved in the body of Christ, not merely the man-made doors of the church as an organization. When people come through Jesus, this door of salvation, they come to know Jesus as the Good Shepherd.

I Am the Good Shepherd

"I am the good shepherd; the good shepherd lays down His life for the sheep" (John 10:11).

This is the sixth "I am" statement of Jesus. Jesus has already established that He is the door through whom people come to salvation. Now He asserts that His work does not end when we cross the threshold but goes on forever. After gathering the flock in a structure or cave for the night, a shepherd lies down in the doorway of the structure or mouth of the cave. His job is to protect. He, in effect, is saying that to get to one of His sheep you must go through Him. Jesus sacrificed His life for our eternal security. He laid down His life for us.

Christians often envision a distorted modern-day picture of a shepherd. We grow up seeing pictures in our churches of an ever-peaceful shepherd boy with a staff in hand, no dirt on him, clean-shaven, no traces of acne, appearing as if he could walk straight out of the pasture into a modern restaurant, slip on a jacket, sit down, and order a meal, with no one thinking he is out of place. In actuality, a shepherd has more in common with a cowboy in the American Wild West. After all, King David bragged, "Your servant has killed both the lion and the bear" (1 Samuel 17:36). Shepherds were tough, gritty, and hard workers who knew about responsibility.

If they lived today, they most likely would be expert marksmen, able to drop a predator from hundreds of yards away.

Because of this distorted view of a shepherd, we often have difficulty envisioning God as tough and gritty, even though Psalm 23 claims that God is our shepherd. He is the one who protects us. In this "I am" statement, Jesus compares Himself to a shepherd, and, in doing so, He further identifies Himself with the Heavenly Father. Specifically, Jesus states that He is the Good Shepherd who lays down His life for His sheep. So the picture we have of Jesus in this passage is of a Savior who gathers those who believe in Him, gives them safe haven, and then lies down in the doorway and basically says to the world, "These people are under my care and provision. I am protecting them." He sacrificed His life in full to ensure our unity with the Father and that our salvation is sealed and eternal. Our assurance of salvation is made possible because of Jesus's power over death.

I Am the Resurrection and the Life

"I am the resurrection and the life; he who believes in Me will live even if he dies, and everyone who lives and believes in Me will never die" (John 11:25–26).

The seventh "I am" statement was spoken in the midst of despair and grief and marks a huge turning point in other people's perception of Jesus and the work He came to do. Mary and Martha were sisters, whose brother, Lazarus, had just died. The story unfolds in John 11. They had sent word several days earlier for Jesus to come because Lazarus was sick. They, along with many people throughout Judea, saw Jesus as a physical healer. They simply viewed Jesus as someone who could make their natural lives better. He gave sight to the blind, healed lepers, healed paralyzed people, and miraculously provided food. Jesus was viewed as someone who had power, but no one realized the extent of that power. This dialogue with Martha revealed the ultimate reason why Jesus was sent by God—to demonstrate that death is no match for Him.

The Pharisees taught about the resurrection of the dead, and many people believed in a resurrection. Jesus narrowed that understanding to claim that the resurrection would come through Him and Him alone. Jesus delayed responding to the request to come to Lazarus's aid to prove His claim as the resurrection and the life.

Lazarus was indeed dead. He had been dead so long that Martha pleaded with Jesus not to remove the stone from the grave because his body had begun to stink. Jesus was in tune with the culture of the day, and He knew the superstitions and beliefs held by the people. For example, they believed the spirit of a person hovered around the dead body for three days. Therefore, by waiting until the fourth day, Jesus ensured this miracle would leave no doubt about His power over death. His power and authority could not be explained away by religious experts, religious leaders, or religious teachers. The miracle of Lazarus's resurrection demonstrates to us that Jesus is completely trustworthy and credible when He states that everyone who believes in Him will never die. When Jesus indwells us, we are spiritually reborn, but unlike our natural birth, which ultimately leads to sickness and death, the spiritual rebirth is eternal. Jesus has to draw us to this rebirth because if it were just up to us, we would delay or deny embracing the life that Jesus offers.

In Genesis 2:16–17, Adam and Eve were told they could eat the fruit of any tree in the garden except one—the tree of knowledge of good and evil. The interesting part of the story is that the tree of life was also there (Genesis 2:9). They could have eaten freely from that tree but ignored it. This is so indicative of humanity. Today, there is a standing invitation to anyone who will believe in Jesus, which is life, but many embrace the inferior and miss out on the spiritual life made possible through Jesus. Spiritual life comes by embracing Jesus as the way, the truth, and the life.

I Am the Way

"I am the way, and the truth, and the life; no one comes to the Father but through Me" (John 14:6).

This "I am" statement is essentially the eighth, ninth, and tenth "I am" statements found in John. It is a continuation of thought that began in John 13:33, where Jesus stated He was getting ready to go to a place where the disciples could not follow Him yet. The statement in John 13:36, "You cannot follow me now", was not the primary emphasis in this initial interaction with His disciples. The primary instruction was, "A new commandment I give to you, that you love one another, even as I have loved you, that you also love one another. By this all men will know that you are My disciples, if you have love for one another" (John 13:34–35). This would later be known as the Law of Christ to which Paul refers in Galatians 6:2. But as is the inclination of almost every human, instead of seizing on the primary instruction that Jesus emphasized, they focused on what they did not understand, that which made them fearful of the future. To address the disciples' fear that they couldn't follow Jesus yet, they were given one of the most beautiful and comforting passages in the Bible, John 14:1–6.

Jesus promises us that He is the *way*. Christians rightly interpret this to mean that Jesus is the way to God, the only way to God. This does not mean that we can lay claim to salvation by uttering Jesus's name like someone would say a magic spell. Nor does it mean that we can merely acknowledge that Jesus is the only way to salvation to receive it. No, this promise goes to a deeper place and realization.

First, "I am the way" is a statement of encouragement. The disciples were confused because Jesus said, "Where I go, you cannot follow Me now; but you will follow later" (John 13:36). They had doubts about the events that were unfolding and were in a general state of bewilderment. Jesus encouraged them to keep the faith and believe that He is the one who leads to God. Christ extends this same assurance to us, in that through trusting Him, we know the Father.

Second, when Jesus states He is the way, He wants the disciples to understand that they will have to go where He goes, the way that He goes. This does not mean they were to all die on a cross. It does mean that they will need to sacrifice, but they will follow Him in sacrifice later. For it is the way Jesus lived, the way He interacted with people, and the way He gave His life as a sacrifice for others that comprises the *way*. Thus, it is incumbent upon everyone wanting to come into a saving knowledge of Jesus Christ to commit to walk in the same manner as He did and be intent on the same purpose as He was (1 John 2:6; Philippians 2:2). Jesus is the *way* to salvation, and we express our salvation and affinity with God by living, interacting, and sacrificing the *way* Christ did.

Paul gives a beautiful understanding of what it means to travel the same way as Jesus, when he instructs the church at Philippi, "Do not merely look out for your own personal interests, but also for the interests of others" (Philippians 2:4). Jesus's "way" was to do the will of God, follow God's plan for His life, and offer Himself as a sacrifice for others—the most wonderful expression of worship in the history of humankind—worship we are to join. Jesus is the means by which we come to the Father, and only by coming to the Father can we experience the truth.

I Am the Truth

Jesus is the truth. Philosophy and science seek to discover truth. Philosophy seeks truth through inductive and deductive reasoning to formulate philosophical arguments. Disciplines such as logic, value theory, metaphysics, and epistemology are used to inform and guide the reasoning process to develop these arguments. Science seeks truth through discovery. The scientific method is utilized to construct hypotheses, use experiments to test the hypotheses, analyze the data, and draw conclusions. Science depends on being able to repeat an experiment and obtain the same results. The Bible doesn't reveal all scientific facts, nor is it confined to use philosophical or scientific frameworks to arrive at truth.

In Hebrew or biblical thought, truth is revealed by God. This is an incredible distinction from the surrounding Greek and Roman culture and philosophy of Jesus's day as well as modern philosophy and scientific discovery. What is critically important to know about God and His relationship to His creation is revealed in Scripture and the person of Jesus Christ. Jesus's character, His love, His compassion, His testimony, and everything He did and said was truth. Jesus not only spoke truth but embodied truth. Karl Barth states, "Revelation is God's self-offering and self-manifestation."[5] Jesus is the full and final revelation of God.

Hebrews 1:1–4 says,

> God, after He spoke long ago to the fathers in the prophets in many portions and in many ways, in these last days has spoken to us in His Son, whom He appointed heir of all things, through whom also He made the world. And He is the radiance of His glory and the exact representation of His nature, and upholds all things by the word of His power. When He had made purification of sins, He sat down at the right hand of the Majesty on high, having become as much better than the angels, as He has inherited a more excellent name than they.

Humankind receives no other testimony about God that surpasses the testimony Jesus embodies concerning God. The beautiful message of the Bible is that Jesus was revealed with the purpose of bringing salvation. To understand the revealed truth that is Jesus, we must be willing to see, and we must be humble.

---

[5] Karl Barth, "The Revelation of God as the Abolition of Religion," in *Christianity and Other Religions: Selected Readings*, ed. John Hick and Brian Hebblethwaite (Philadelphia: Fortress Press, 1980), 36.

By design, this gift is objectionable when viewed through only a human lens. God still requires humility of spirit to see His gift, its claims on our lives, and its power to transform us. The challenge is to set aside our demand that all truth be reasoned through the framework of philosophy or discovered through science. Humanity has been presented with revealed truth through Jesus Christ. It takes faith to embrace the revealed truth of Jesus.

Just as the disciples had to come to an encounter with Jesus that allowed them to "see" the truth, so do we. They had trouble getting beyond their own culturally ingrained understanding of who the Messiah would be and what He would do to liberate people. The gospel is a message of liberation but of spiritual, not necessarily physical, liberation. This liberation delivers us from spiritual darkness and is expressed by practicing the truth (John 3:21). It allows people to experience God in truth, not uncertainty; truth, not obscurity; truth, not manipulation. We must avoid letting philosophy and science keep us from experiencing freedom. The message of John 13:34 is that our lives give testimony to the truth by loving as Jesus loves us. In that way we become a part of the legacy of revelation, of truth. Following Jesus as the way and the truth leads to life.

I Am the Life

"I am the life" in John 14:6 is the tenth "I am" statement. It is not merely a repetition of Jesus's seventh "I am" statement when Jesus raised Lazarus from the dead. The resurrection of Lazarus demonstrated Jesus's power *over* death. This "I am" statement, found in John 14:6, showed Jesus's power *through* death.

This brings further clarity to Jesus's statement that the disciples couldn't follow Him right now but would later. In this conversation with the disciples, Christ reveals one of the great ironies in the Christian faith. Jesus's death brings life, and our relinquishing control of our destinies and agendas brings us life. In other words, dying to our dogged determination to live the way we want brings abundant life. However, it is crucial to remember that we can't die to ourselves, according to our own thinking or even according to what the world accepts as an "appropriate" act of selflessness. It must be with the same dedication as Jesus, offering oneself in a life of worship—of sacrifice, as Jesus modeled and taught. "If anyone wishes to come after Me, he must deny himself, and take up his cross and follow Me. For whoever wishes to save his life will lose it; but whoever loses his life for My sake will find it" (Matthew 16:24–25).

Jesus invites us to enter into life through death—His death on the Cross and our death to a self-determined life. Embracing Jesus as "the way, and the truth, and the life" is the process where we come to abide in Jesus. This is the only way to ensure our lives produce something of eternal significance—spiritual fruit.

I Am the Vine

"I am the true vine, and My Father is the vinedresser" (John 15:1). "I am the vine, you are the branches; he who abides in Me and I in him, he bears much fruit, for apart from Me you can do nothing" (John 15:5).

The outcome of coming to the Father through Jesus Christ as the way, and the truth, and the life is a vital union with Jesus that bears fruit. This *is* abiding in Christ. Jesus is in union with God. "Believe Me that I am in the Father and the Father is in Me" (John 14:11). Jesus does nothing outside the will of the Father, and God does His work and speaks through Jesus. They abide in one another, and their wills are one. They have an unshakable and eternal affinity for and with one another. In the same way, we are wed to Jesus Christ and His will. Our entire lives are given to bear the fruit that Jesus is at work preparing and bringing to fruition in us.

Jesus describes God as the vinedresser, removing branches that have no hope of bearing fruit and pruning the ones that bear fruit so they can bear more fruit (John 15:1–4). When we abide in Jesus, it is readily evident through our lives, and there is never any danger of not producing fruit. We cannot bear spiritual fruit unless we are wed to Jesus and abide in Him and His character, life, and sacrifice; unless we abide in Him through His way, His truth, and His life.

Many Christians often experience frustration in their faith because they try to abide in Jesus through the strength of their own wills and possibly through their own hard work. They seek to earn favor with God by accumulating a lot of accomplishments and good works and bringing them to God seeking His validation and acceptance. Abiding in Christ is the acknowledgment that we are validated because of our relationship with Him, because we came to the Father through Him.

Now, we do not bear fruit outside that relationship and validation but because of it. We experience the intentionally, dynamically present Christ by being connected to Him. This allows us to bear spiritual fruit. In order to bear that fruit, we must commit ourselves to the preparations necessary to live life as we are called to live it. The only chance we have of doing this is to abide in the living God.

Jesus, the Son of the Living God demonstrated through His life what worship in Spirit and truth looks like, inviting us to commit our lives in worship. But it is not a worship that calls us to withdraw from the world to create a false security and shelter. We find shelter in the Savior, in His companionship, doing His work. He is the Good Shepherd. We carry on the worship He began by offering our lives in sacrifice. This sacrifice is not for our sake, but for the sake of the world, bringing people to the redeeming work of God through Jesus Christ. Jesus extends an invitation to us to join Him in the work of redemption. This is the divine worship to which we have been called.

PART 3

FIRST ACTS
OF WORSHIP

CHAPTER 6

THE GREAT COMMISSION— OUR CALL TO WORSHIP

"All authority has been given to Me in heaven and on earth. Go therefore and make disciples of all the nations, baptizing them in the name of the Father, and the Son, and the Holy Spirit, teaching them to observe all that I commanded you; and lo, I am with you always, even to the end of the age" (Matthew 28:18–20).

The Great Commission is Christ's final command and our call to worship. It is the culmination of Jesus's life and teachings— how He prepared His followers to become disciples and thereby make disciples. The first thing to notice is that Jesus possesses all authority to commission us. His authority is based on His name, His character—who He is as God's Son. In His authority, He sends us with a specific purpose. That purpose is to make disciples.

In the original Greek language, the word translated *make disciples* is from the Greek word *matheteusate* and is the only imperative verb in the Great Commission. The words *go, baptizing,* and *teaching* are participles. This doesn't take away from the urgency and imperative force of *go, baptizing, and teaching*, but they are the "how to" of our ultimate purpose: to make disciples. The three participles are the way we make mature followers of Jesus Christ.

Our commission is more than proclamation, trying to persuade people to become Christians and baptizing them; this is commonly referred to as evangelism. Evangelism, as normally practiced, fulfills only part of the Great Commission. Our work is not done when someone believes and is baptized. While it's incredibly important to carrying out the Great Commission, the modern American implementation and fulfillment of the Great Commission often begins and ends with persuasion and baptism. Evangelism is where the Great Commission begins, not where it ends. We leave in our wake immature Christians if our mission fails to encompass all three participles. A biblically centered Great Commission fully encompasses the practice and process of making disciples including going, baptizing, and teaching. People who only want to be involved in proclamation and persuasion neglect the common call Jesus has given to every Christian to make disciples. So evangelists must make sure they are involved in the complete fulfillment of the Great Commission.

Likewise, there is no room for someone to neglect the call to proclaim the gospel and persuade others to become a Christian so they can focus on "discipleship". This doesn't mean that when a Christian leads another person to commit his or her life to Christ that the new convert can only be taught by the person who was instrumental in him or her coming to faith in Jesus. Nor does it mean that you can't disciple a person another Christian has led to commit his or her life to Christ. In 1 Corinthians 3:6 Paul writes, "I planted, Apollos watered, but God was causing the growth." So, making disciples is a team effort, but every member of the team participates in "evangelism" and "discipleship".

Every Christian who desires to fulfill the Great Commission must model all three participles or he or she is not actually involved in discipleship. They are merely meeting with people and having religious discussions. Discipleship includes modeling a bold verbal witness for Jesus for those you are trying to disciple. The apostle Paul is a superior example of this encompassing command involving what we commonly refer to as evangelism and discipleship. He was a dedicated evangelist as evidenced by starting churches throughout the known world. He was also a disciple maker by molding Timothy into a mature follower of Jesus, but his discipleship included evangelism. He told Timothy, "Do the work of an evangelist" (2 Timothy 4:5).

Disciple making is not automatic and takes concerted effort by individuals and churches. To make disciples, we must teach people the specific curriculum of Christ. We fulfill the command known as the Great Commission by teaching others to observe all the commands of Jesus which equips them to proclaim the gospel by how they live and speak. The commands of Jesus are the most challenging set of teachings in history. Observing them and teaching others to observe them takes a high level of commitment. The Christian is required to set aside hatred for love, cynicism for hope, revenge for forgiveness, fear for courage, and worry for faith, among many other actions. It requires us to deny ourselves and follow Christ, no matter the cost, seeking our spiritual nourishment from the appropriation of His sacrifice. Keeping the commands is our outpouring of worship.

This becomes a problem because many Christians are never taught the specific commands of Christ. I was tempted, when writing this book, to merely state that we should teach others to observe the commands of Jesus without explaining them in these pages. It would have made for a much shorter book but may have facilitated a tacit approval to not take them as seriously as we should and ignore their centrality in the deepening of our Christian lives and fulfillment of the Great Commission. Ultimately, I concluded we must become more than merely aware of the commands of Christ because in order to teach them, we must both know and practice them. They must be grafted into every aspect of our lives of worship.

This doesn't mean that only the most knowledgeable Christians are fit for disciple making or that we must be perfect. If that were the case we would all be disqualified. We do need to stay, however, a little ahead of those we are teaching in order to help them realize what they should strive for in their desire to know God and fulfill His purpose for their lives. This requires that the commands of Jesus be so engrained in our lives that we easily and naturally demonstrate them as we explain them. We now turn our attention to the commands of Jesus—our means of worship. We begin where Jesus began: with repentance and belief.

Repent and Believe

"The time is fulfilled, and the kingdom of God is at hand; repent and believe in the gospel" (Mark 1:15; cf. Matthew 4:17).

Repentance is required. Jesus withdrew to Galilee and began to preach after He overcame the temptation of Satan in the desert. Often, Jesus isn't thought of as a preacher, but He took up the work that John the Baptist had begun. Many people acknowledge Jesus as a teacher, healer, or prophet. Preaching, however, was the first avenue Jesus used to begin His ministry of transformation in the hearts of men and women. Jesus consistently preached repentance, His first command. Repentance was the subject of His first sermon and was His first instruction to us.

The word *repent* means an "about-face" or "going in the opposite direction" with our lives. This has powerful implications. When we hear the word *repent*, we immediately think of repenting of our sins. In other words, we want to find forgiveness for our sins in Christ Jesus. What we miss in this call to repent of our sins is the chance to leave the desire to sin. We are not only repenting of our "sins"—those wrong things we have done in life—but we are repenting of our "Sin"—the direction of our lives that comes as a result of human nature. Jesus calls us to step forward in belief that He has the power to change our corrupted human nature, providing a new direction in which to live.

Jesus's provision of grace is the beautiful aspect of His dynamic preaching. Believing that Jesus is the Savior of humankind is the first step in moving in a different direction in life after we repent and turn our backs on the old direction of our lives. It would have been fundamentally cruel to preach the need of repentance from sin, bring an awareness that everyone is moving in the wrong direction, and then leave us to search for the way to live. Christians experience frustration and fatigue in the journey of faith if repentance consists only of asking and receiving forgiveness of sins because we feel guilty for what we have done. Life becomes constant defeat, always repenting of what we do wrong but never embracing what it takes to live right and move forward in a new direction.

Just as it does physically, constantly turning 180 degrees spiritually results in moving only in a circle, going nowhere, and often ending in the same condition and place where we started. Judgmental attitudes or giving up are often the outcomes of one-sided cyclical repentance. God promises a new path for our transformed lives. We are not called to just turn but to step forward after we turn. The process of repentance and belief leads us to spiritual rebirth.

Be Born Again

"Truly, truly, I say to you, unless one is born of water and the Spirit he cannot enter into the kingdom of God ... Do not be amazed that I said to you, 'You must be born again.'" (John 3:5, 7).

In John 3, we find the story of Nicodemus and his conversation with Jesus about being *born again* or *born from above*. This is one of the most common passages used by evangelicals to show the need for personal salvation. The term "born again" is a powerful image of the requirement of transformation. We must be born of the Spirit to be transformed or "born again".

John 3:16–21 says,

> For God so loved the world, that He gave His only
> begotten Son, that whoever believes in Him shall not
> perish, but have eternal life. For God did not send His
> Son into the world to judge the world, but that the world
> might be saved through Him. He who believes in Him
> is not judged; he who does not believe has been judged
> already, because he has not believed in the name of the
> only begotten Son of God. This is the judgment, that
> the Light has come into the world, and men loved the
> darkness rather than the Light, for their deeds were
> evil. For everyone who does evil hates the Light, and
> does not come to the Light for fear that his deeds will
> be exposed. But he who practices the truth comes to the
> Light, so that his deeds may be manifested as having
> been wrought in God.

Those who do evil reject the Light of Jesus. Those who practice the truth are drawn to the Light (John 3:21). Jesus's statements in John 3 reveal that God is at work in us prior to our encounter with the Light and our subsequent salvation. This passage merely points out that Jesus's judgment is based on belief, and those people who come to belief are drawn to the Light (Jesus) because their deeds reveal a heart desiring God. Conversely, those who are involved in evil deeds reveal their hearts, which is evidenced by rejecting Jesus. This teaching of Jesus about light and darkness corresponds to the story of Cornelius in chapter 10 of the book of Acts.

Cornelius was a devout, God-fearing man and a person who did good works by giving alms to the Jews; he prayed to God continually. He was told through a vision to send some of his men to Joppa to get Simon (Peter). The next day, Peter was praying and was told to accompany these men without misgivings. Cornelius listened to Peter proclaim the gospel, committed his life to Jesus, and was baptized. His story demonstrates that a man who fears God,

who does good deeds, and whose heart is open to God accepts the
message of Jesus and His salvation upon hearing it. A heart holding
to and embracing acts of evil and that is closed to God will reject
the gospel. Whether or not a person is involved in acts of good or
evil does not alter what is needed in both types of people—the
transformation of the heart through new birth in Jesus Christ, a
life in the Spirit. It is through coming to Jesus for transformation
through salvation that confirms that the good works someone did
were wrought, or worked, in God (John 3:21).

We evangelicals throw around the phrase "born again" but seem
to lack an understanding of its significance. It is not a phrase to be
taken lightly. It is not to be used to align ourselves with political or
theological conservatives, deluding ourselves into thinking it places
us in the religious camp of people who truly understand Scripture
above all other concepts and understandings of our faith. The phrase
born again is simply a statement of truth by Jesus. The statement of
truth asserts that one must be born-again (John 3:3)—alternately
described as born of water and the spirit—or he or she cannot see or
enter into the kingdom of God. *Born again* means to enter into new
life, and is one of the most important truths of the Christian faith.

This is something that is so difficult for some in our day—and
some of the people in Jesus's day—to comprehend. We demand to
see, to have proof, to be shown a sign before belief. Jesus said, "A
sign will not be given to this generation" (Matthew 16:4; cf. Mark
8:12). God desires for us to be sensitive to His "wooing" us. We truly
have to be open-minded and open-hearted to recognize the pursuit
in which God is engaged to bring us to the point of faith. The God
who pursues us is also drawing us through the ministry of the Holy
Spirit. Up to this point, we cannot see or enter the kingdom of God;
we can only see or hear about the Son of God, Jesus Christ. Those
who are open-minded and open-hearted are drawn to Jesus Christ,
the Light. When we believe and have faith in Jesus Christ as God's
Son, we are born of the Spirit, or born again.

Every human is born of water through his or her natural birth. Only those who believe in Jesus are reborn. However, to experience this rebirth requires that we realize we are spiritually impoverished. "Blessed are the poor in spirit, for theirs is the kingdom of heaven" (Matthew 5:3). The recognition of spiritual poverty is essential to a relationship with God. Regardless of whether we are involved in evil deeds and slinking toward deeper darkness and self-degradation or we are involved in good deeds, there must come a time when we recognize our need for spiritual rebirth.

This can't be confused with merely satisfaction in life; it is something more. Recognition of spiritual poverty is the first stepping stone to spiritual life. When we are arrogant and prideful, discounting our spiritual poverty, we respond to the truth with anger, manifested in hostility to Jesus, His followers, and the gospel. Humility, even the humility to admit we need spiritual rebirth and we don't fully understand God or His ways, is essential to taking the step into new life. This is indispensable for salvation.

Christians who understand this reaction of anger based on pride can easily comprehend the common reactions from those throughout the world when they are told they need Jesus to bring salvation to their lives. When the truth is proclaimed that Jesus is the only way to salvation, it reveals a man's or woman's heart. He or she either retreats into darkness, is drawn to consider the light, or embraces the light. Those who retreat into darkness may engage in a new expression of evil, and that is to try to destroy children of the Light—Christians. Those who are drawn to Jesus confirm that the good works that they have done have been worked in God and then join Christians in the greatest work of God—redemption.

Lest one conclude that I am suggesting someone is or can be justified by works, let me clarify. The story of Cornelius and this entire section screams just the opposite. Regardless of whether our deeds are classified as evil or good, or if our hearts are closed or open to God, we are justified by faith in Jesus and Jesus alone—by His grace (Ephesians 2:8–9). If someone can be justified by works or by a pre-Christian faith, there would have been no reason for God to speak to Peter and Cornelius in different dreams—one for Cornelius to send for Peter, and, in the other dream, for Peter to go to Cornelius. The gospel is not a litmus test for preexisting faith. It is the transformative power of God, found exclusively in the person of Jesus Christ.

Again, Cornelius is described as a God-fearer, a person who did good deeds. And he wasn't the only one. The book of Acts says that Cornelius and all his household feared God and gave alms, which most likely included his wife, children, and servants. This story demonstrates the sufficient faithfulness of God, not the possibility of a sufficient preexisting faith. God will not leave people stranded in belief in Him, doing good works without revealing salvation to them or sending someone to proclaim Jesus Christ and His life, death, and resurrection.

This conclusion is also supported by the story of Philip in the book of Acts. Philip was told to go down to the road that leads to Gaza, where he found an Ethiopian eunuch who was reading the prophet Isaiah, searching for answers (Acts 8:26–31). Both of these stories negate that "red-herring" hypothetical question that is thrown in the face of Christians: "What about the person who has never heard of Jesus?" This question speaks more to a person's low view of God's character and lack of confidence in His love and mercy. God is faithful to call and send His people to give testimony of Jesus to those who need Him and are ready and searching for Him. Those who hear must respond with humble belief, like a child.

Like a Child

"Let the children alone, and do not hinder them from coming to Me; for the kingdom of heaven belongs to such as these" (Matthew 19:14; cf. Matthew 18:3–6, 10; Mark 10:14–15; Luke 18:16–17).

These verses of Scripture show us the heart of God. Five separate commands deal with children and their place with God in His kingdom. We see God's love toward those whom society dismisses. The gospel, or good news, is for every person in the entire world, including children, bidding them to choose God through the person of Jesus Christ. There is no exclusive club inside the kingdom of God. The church and its ministers must never communicate through words or actions that status in the kingdom of God is based on the same criteria as status and prestige in the world. Children bring no expectation of special status, nor do they have any awareness of inferiority based on family heritage. They come to Jesus without any ulterior motive. They desire only relationship.

The world esteems people who are born into wealth and privilege or people who, by their own hard work and tenacity, earn their status. The gospel speaks against such status in the kingdom of God. James 2:1–4 testifies to this when James tells Christians,

> My brethren, do not hold your faith in our glorious Lord Jesus Christ with an attitude of personal favoritism. For if a man comes into your assembly with a gold ring and dressed in fine clothes, and there also comes in a poor man in dirty clothes, and you pay special attention to the one who is wearing the fine clothes, and say, 'You sit here in a good place,' and you say to the poor man, 'you stand over there, or sit down by my footstool,' have you not made distinctions among yourselves, and become judges with evil motives?

Jesus says, "Do not judge according to appearance, but judge with righteous judgment" (John 7:24). Jesus and the writers of the New Testament were consistent in their proclamation that God is no respecter of persons. God looks at the heart of a man or woman and expects us to do so as well. What Jesus wants to see in us is the heart of a child. Coming to Christ as a child protects us from pride and prepares us to follow Jesus.

Follow

"Follow Me, and I will make you fishers of men" (Matthew 4:19; cf. Mark 1:17).

We do not have a record of how long Jesus went from city to city preaching repentance, but He became well known. This is evident because when He asked Peter and Andrew, John and James, and Nathaniel and Philip to follow Him, they did not ask Jesus who He was; they immediately followed. They were not told where they were going but what they were going to do. The road map they were given for life was a person—Jesus Christ.

The grace of God does not merely "baptize" our self-determined way of living and hope it becomes God's will. Salvation requires a path in a different direction with a different outcome. This outcome leads us, just as it did the disciples, to see God, His work, His will, the world, and our lives in a completely different light. Following Jesus brings a new perception. Some perceptions change because we grow in intellect and leave behind childlike reasoning.

When Annelise, our second child, was three years old, she asked me a question one evening after she had taken a bath. She held up her yellow rubber duck and asked, "Daddy, do ducks sleeps sitting up, or do they sleeps on thems sides?" I replied, "Well, Sweetie, ducks spend all their time in the water or on the shore when they are not flying, so I guess they sleep sitting up." She replied, as she turned abruptly and marched to her room, head rocking from side to side, "Daddy don't know. Ducks don't sleeps in thems water or on thems shores; they sleeps in thems beds." It was a logical conclusion for her. She always slept in beds and everyone she knew slept in beds. Wouldn't it make sense that all people and animals would sleep in beds also? I am happy to say that she has developed a higher level of reasoning as she has matured.

Christian maturity moves beyond the natural maturity common to all men and women. It moves us to think of the world beyond merely our own experiences. We stop demanding that everything be based on our perspectives. Following Jesus is two different experiences at the same time. It is a walk into the most secure setting and a walk into the most tumultuous setting, simultaneously. The security is the Savior, Christ Jesus. The tumult is the redefinition or transformation of our lives and perspectives.

Jesus approached the first disciples to follow Him while they were doing their jobs as hardworking fishermen. When the disciples left their nets for Jesus, they retained some of their former gifts, skills, and personalities when they repented, believed, and followed, but those gifts, skills, and personalities would be used for a new purpose. The values and traits they developed as fishermen, such as hard work, tenacity, competition, connection to the common person, and business acumen would serve them well in their new calling. They would still be fishermen, but they would be catching something much more important—people. First, Jesus would need to reprogram their understanding of what religion and religious expression looked like so they would be able to embody the New Covenant as well as explain it.

Jesus has the same plan in store for us. He meets us as we are, with the talents and skills we possess. He then gives us spiritual gifts to transform our talents and skills to use for His kingdom (Romans 12:6–8; 1 Corinthians 12:4–11, 28). These gifts are used in our everyday lives for spiritual significance and eternal purpose when we humble ourselves to His work in our hearts, step out in faith to follow Him, and seek to embody His teachings with our lives.

Seek

"Ask, and it will be given to you; seek, and you will find; knock, and it will be opened to you" (Luke 11:9; Matthew 7:7). "But seek first His kingdom and His righteousness, and all these things will be added to you" (Matthew 6:33).

Ask can also be translated as *beg*. One of the misconceptions about faith in God through Jesus Christ is that we merely have to believe there is a God and believe in the facts of Jesus's life to find and live in salvation. But when Jesus imparts salvation to us, it is not a permission slip to be lazy. It ushers in a desire to know more about Jesus and His plan for life. Jesus begins the process of transformation in our lives when we repent, believe, and accept His forgiveness and salvation. This transformation is discovered; rather, it is given to those who desire it and who seek it.

Many people, however, do not seek transformation by God; they seek tangible security for their lives and view God as a means to that security. This common misconception about salvation stresses mere recognition of God rather than holy reverence and submission to Him. Church leaders are at their best when they equip Christians to offer their lives to God in their entirety and trust He will not only secure their salvation but transform them.

If church leaders create a false religious security, it infects their congregations and corrupts the true message of the gospel, from a self-sacrificing message to a self-centered message. When people seek salvation without transformation, sacrifice, or a desire to truly know and be known by God, it reveals a heart seeking security, rather than God's will. People are often misled to buy into Grace because it promises eternal security for their souls. It's the mind-set of fearing hell or "better safe than sorry." This desire for eternal security is then translated to a belief that God will make them secure on this earth as well. They are misled to pray for prosperity and that God will grant them all the desires of their hearts, whether or not their desires are aligned with His. This is extremely dangerous because it leads people farther away from God. They become enslaved to the false religious security, never experiencing the freedom of boldly walking with Christ.

We, as believers after God's heart, yearn above all else to come to the truth, to know the truth, and be set free by the truth. We do not seek security for our lives but rather trust the Father with our lives. We seek to enter into His understanding and view of the world. We strive for what nourishes our souls—a life connected to God in sacrifice.

Strive

"Strive to enter through the narrow door; for many, I tell you, will seek to enter and will not be able" (Luke 13:24). "Enter through the narrow gate; for the gate is wide and the way is broad that leads to destruction, and there are many who enter through it" (Matt. 7:13).

These verses reveal a requirement from people regarding the Christian faith that runs the gamut of the complexity of human nature. Some people look to attain only a life of comfort and ease. Others seek and strive for a life of austerity and self-denial, some because of religious devotion. It is not enough to live a life of devotion if it is not done for the right cause and belief. Jesus demonstrated the narrow way through His life. He followed the narrow way by taking on the character of God and demonstrating the mercy and love of God through a life of dedicated sacrifice, which fulfilled the purpose and will of God for Jesus's life. Jesus implores His followers to follow the narrow way, marked by self-denial and sacrifice but not a self-sacrifice and denial only for our "spiritual" connection with God but for the sake of others.

At this stage of spiritual growth and understanding a Christian is ready to enter into a relationship with Jesus that opens up new vistas of call and purpose for life. This is where the person who is making disciples has the opportunity to lead the new Christian into understanding and committing to an unparalleled opportunity—to set aside self and become a new creature in Christ Jesus. In many cases, the new Christian is brought to the point of seeking and striving to enter into a deep affinity with the person, character, and ministry of Jesus—and then a bait-and-switch takes place.

The Christian is taught a formula of growing in knowledge of Jesus Christ that is merely an intellectual assimilation of facts about Jesus. He or she is taught to spend a certain amount of time in prayer each day, memorize Scripture, and witness to non-Christians through this formula-based plan. Discipleship is not a formula of Scripture memory, prayer, and witnessing that takes place apart from observing the commands of Jesus. Scripture memory, prayer, and witnessing take place while the Christian is taught and shown how to observe the commands of Christ. When these commands permeate our lives, prayer and Scripture then become an empowering of the disciple to engage the world in a powerful witness—to become worshipers.

CHAPTER 7

COMMITMENT IN WORSHIP

"If anyone wishes to come after Me, he must deny himself, and take up his cross daily and follow Me" (Luke 9:23; cf. Matthew 16:24).

Following Jesus is difficult. The church speaks frequently about sacrifice and service, as it should. But trying to demonstrate a committed life without first denying oneself is futile. We must let go of our self-satisfied lives, thinking that the life we plan and lay out for ourselves is sufficient. Down deep, maybe we think that God is kind of lucky to have people involved in the church who are as talented, educated, or polished as we are. We take pride in our achievements. We relish the accolades that come our way and even begin to scheme in our hearts how to bring even more attention to ourselves, all the while putting on a façade of humility. A committed life without denial has all the appearances of living a life identified with Christ Jesus, but it really just becomes an exercise in futility—a grand deception of others and ourselves.

Jesus calls us to deny ourselves. We set aside our obsessions and preoccupations of using our gifts and talents to build our names, champion our interests, and protect our religious turf. We take up our crosses, which are "our calling and purpose," as a true sacrifice offered to God. This is the only way to fulfill the call to follow Jesus for God's interests. This may seem like too much of a load to carry, but Jesus stands ready to assist us.

Come and Learn

"Come to Me, all who are weary and heavy laden, and I will give you rest. Take My yoke upon you and learn from Me, for I am gentle and humble in heart, and you will find rest for your souls. For My yoke is easy and My burden is light" (Matthew 11:28–30).

The verbs *come, take,* and *learn* are imperatives. Again, the context enhances the meaning of the commands. Jesus had just reprimanded the residents of the cities where he had worked miracles and proclaimed to them that if they had been gentiles they would have repented. The cities in Israel were still bound by the tradition of the Law and could not embrace Jesus as the Messiah. The people were weighed down by the Law which led them to reject God's messengers regardless of who He sent to them. John the Baptist and Jesus used entirely different means to proclaim God's salvation, but the people rejected both of them (Matthew 11:18-19).

Sin is a heavy burden. Trying to alleviate sin by following a bunch of rules is an even heavier load to bear. People who try to work their way into God's grace are among the most tragic people in the world. They never get to experience release from sin, nor freedom in Christ. Many will eventually escape the constraints of the Law by giving up, tired of feeling guilty, and living how they want to. This is a false deliverance.

Jesus's deliverance offers hope of a lighter load in life. He removes the burden of sin and the Law. He commands people to *come* to Him. Keeping the Law as the religious leaders prescribed was keeping people from following God. But escaping the Law does not give us a life free from constraints. We can't correct the mistake of trying to earn grace by works, only to replace it with an equally grave mistake and that is to jettison every restraint and live a life of immorality or selfish ambition. Jesus commands us to *take* His yoke upon us.

On a farm, a yoke is made for two animals to enable them to pull heavier loads together than they can apart. Grace doesn't invite us to live an unconstrained life, but a life in partnership with Jesus, working for the same purpose as He is working. Jesus's yoke is easy and light because our hearts are joined with His heart in grace and love. We are free to live with Christ.

The last imperative is *learn*. When we partner with Jesus He doesn't leave us alone. He teaches us. We study His life. We observe others who follow Him and learn how to become a disciple. When we become a disciple of Jesus we find rest for our souls. We are content.

Our lives offered as worship to God will become a burden too great to bear if we try to do it alone. The comfort is that we don't have to bear the burden alone. Jesus has instructed us to rely on Him. There are some things in life that we are just not capable of doing entirely in our own strength, and one of them is to live the life Jesus intends for us. There is no shame or guilt in realizing that a challenge is too difficult to face on our own. Jesus understands this better than anyone.

Jesus experienced this in the Garden of Gethsemane the night before His death. He asked the disciples to share his load by praying for Him. He submitted His will to the will of His Father, no matter the cost. Also, when Jesus was bearing the Cross on His back on the road to the crucifixion, He couldn't go any further. Simon of Cyrene had to be enlisted to carry the Cross for Him (Matthew 27:32). Jesus is uniquely qualified to bear our burdens.

We are going to face some mountains that are just too steep for us to walk on our own as we discover what a sacrificial life entails. It is crucial that we prepare for this by being yoked with Jesus in the smaller burdens of life. This pattern of trust develops faith in us so we can trust Him when the most difficult challenges come our way. This submission is the yoke of Jesus, aligning ourselves with the will of Christ and being set free from the hopeless effort to live life according to the Law or the will of others.

Our roles and relationships are the only things that give us unique, tangible meaning in life. When these roles are redefined, refocused, and recommitted in Christ, there will be some upheaval, doubts, and maybe even some despair as the ultimate climax of our worship comes into focus. Jesus knew this. He prepared for this. Jesus assists us to bear every burden, lightening the load and weight of worry, fret, and religious performance. We join Him in a life of sacrifice, knowing His spirit is always with us, empowering us. We have many roles and traits in life, but they are all to be realigned to God's purpose as our crosses to bear, yoked with Jesus, as we live a life of devoted sacrifice.

Singular Devotion

"If anyone comes to Me, and does not hate his own father and mother and wife and children and brothers and sisters, yes, and even his own life, he cannot be My disciple" (Luke 14:26).

It appears Jesus's command to hate our family and our very existence stands in contradiction to the overall message of the Bible, the teachings of Jesus concerning love, and the character of God. Again, Christ emphasizes the denial of self, using a stronger word: hate. When I first quoted this verse to my children, their first response was, "I thought you weren't supposed to hate anyone if you are a Christian." This is one of those verses that is initially confusing. It requires a fuller understanding and explanation.

The parallel passage of Scripture for Luke 14:26 is Matthew 10:37, which says, "He who loves father or mother more than Me in not worthy of Me; and he who loves son or daughter more than Me is not worthy of Me." Taken together, these passages teach us that every other relationship in life is now defined through Christ. His agenda for our lives takes precedence over every other agenda anyone else places on us, even our own agenda.

Jesus uses the word *hate* in the Luke passage. The passage leads us to conclude that Jesus was not speaking of a visceral kind of hatred that wants to see personal destruction. This would make no practical sense, as we are told we must hate our own lives. The passage means that other people's plans for our lives must be ignored and put away. It is only Jesus's call that matters. Matthew states it in the positive. We must love Jesus's agenda and plans for life more than all the plans others have for us, even more than the plans we have for ourselves. His agenda demands urgency.

Urgent Response

"Follow Me, and allow the dead to bury their own dead" (Matthew 8:22).

When we receive an invitation to a party, we are expected to give an RSVP by a certain date. The call for every Christian to follow Jesus and offer his or her life as worship to God demands urgency. We do not have the luxury of taking care of those things that are merely cultural expectations or personal interests, while putting off our response to God's purpose in life until it suits us. The sacrifice of worship begins immediately. As a husband, mother, employee, student, or professional, we follow Jesus—now.

The context of this verse of Scripture is a man who wanted to go home and wait for his father to die. He wanted to return to take care of worldly concerns first. He failed to see the urgency of the call. He wanted to secure a safety net for himself. This man probably wanted to ensure that he received a monetary inheritance. Once that security was in place, he would follow Jesus. We must depend completely on Jesus when He calls us, letting go of earthly securities. We must commit all that we have and all that we are in following Christ.

Work for Spiritual Food

"Do not work for the food which perishes, but for the food which endures to eternal life, which the Son of Man will give to you, for on Him the Father, God, has set His seal" (John 6:27).

Jesus found His nourishment in doing the will of God (John 4:35). The will of God for Jesus was a journey to the Cross, the culmination and ultimate expression and testimony of how Jesus's entire life had been lived. Jesus was determined to go to Jerusalem (Luke 9:51, 53). He was fully aware of God's plan and call on His life—a life that ultimately led to His death. His life was given to this journey of sacrifice. This was the food that gave Him nourishment—the food that never spoils, but is eternal. Jesus commands us to keep our eyes on that which is truly important and that partaking of the food that is eternal will bring the contentment we long for.

Desire True Treasures

"Do not store up for yourselves treasures on earth, where moth and rust destroy, and where thieves break in and steal. But store up for yourselves treasures in heaven" (Matthew 6:19–20).

Life involves pursuit. We strive for something. We work to accumulate for ourselves the things we treasure. There are many ways to store up treasures on earth. The most obvious is the acquisition of money, but this command immediately follows Jesus's instructions on avoiding public shows of religious devotion.

Wealth is not the only worldly treasure that bids for our energies and talents. We are also tempted to seek the treasures of notoriety, acclaim, and recognition. But the treasures we are to strive for are unseen and unnoticed most of the time. They do not demand public acknowledgement, awards, or applause from crowds. The treasures for which we strive are the works of God in the lives of people. The challenge is to treasure the same thing God treasures, which is seeing people become faithful followers of Jesus. For this to be possible, we must give to God what we are inviting others to give to God, and that is our lives.

Give Our Lives to God

"Then render to Caesar the things that are Caesar's; and to God the things that are God's" (Matthew 22:21; cf. Mark 12:17; Luke 20:25).

In this one command is summarized the affinity that worldly wealth has in relation to power, in contrast to the affinity of true treasures. Money has nearly always had the image of a leader of a country on it. In this way, money is a symbol of the authority that is derived by human over human. On the other hand, we, God's created beings, are a symbol of the living God. We are stamped by His ownership and handiwork—created in His image—by His authority.

The Pharisees were scheming and attempting to trap Jesus in aligning Himself as a friend of the Roman government, thereby ruining His credibility with the people, or speaking against paying a tax that would allow them to accuse Jesus of treason. They thought they had Jesus in a conundrum because they didn't have a proper view of money and wealth. They saw the tax as the Roman government's taking something that rightfully belonged to them. However, if they had seen money not as a possession to be taken from them but as a resource God uses to advance His work, the religious leaders wouldn't have been so surprised by Jesus's response. The greatest resources God uses to advance His work are people.

This is illustrative of deeper problems with the entire religious culture they had constructed. To them, religion was a tool to use as leverage on the people and on God. The people would conform because of the traditions and teachings that had been a part of their lives during their generation, as well as for many generations before them. They thought that God had no other choice but to bless them and fulfill their desire to see the throne of David restored because they were the sons of Abraham, the chosen of God. Because of their spiritual blindness, however, they missed entirely that the beginning of spiritual blessing and abundant life is to give one's life to God—no strings attached and no other loyalties.

We render to God our lives offered in their entirety as a sacrifice for His use, and because of this, money ceases to be our master. We render to God our bodies and personalities that He created so that they can become the transformed images of Jesus. Money and possessions are merely two of the means that God uses to advance His work in His true treasures—people. When we embrace this change in life—a heart that is conformed into the image of Christ— we can truly live a life dedicated to God and God alone.

CHAPTER 8

PERSONAL DEDICATION IN WORSHIP

"And he who does not take his cross and follow after Me is not worthy of Me" (Matthew 10:38).

"Fifty-nine, sixty, sixty-one, sixty-two—jog a lap." Mr. Jack Miller was our track and cross-country coach. He stood just inside the track and calmly called out these numbers as we finished each quarter mile run during our workouts. Sometimes, we would run twelve laps or, every so often, sixteen laps on the days of the quarter-mile workouts, always jogging a lap or walking a half a lap between. Occasionally, as we would start the next quarter mile, he would calmly and softly say, "Train to run; run to win." This phrase stuck in my head.

Paul states in 1 Corinthians 9:24-27:

> "Do you not know that those who run in a race all run, but only one receives the prize? Run in such a way that you may win. Everyone who competes in the games exercises self-control in all things. They then do it to receive a perishable wreath, but we an imperishable. Therefore I run in such a way, as not without aim; I box

in such a way, as not beating the air; but I discipline my
body and make it my slave, so that, after I have preached
to others, I myself will not be disqualified."

Upon first reading the above passage of Scripture, it seems that
the only emphasis is on winning a race, and one might wrongly
conclude that we are in competition with other Christians when
it comes to living the Christian faith. But the emphasis is about
the training it takes to enter the competition against the Evil One,
Satan. Without the training, there is no chance of spiritual victory.

This is a reference to the Isthmian Games in ancient Greece.
These and the ancient Olympics were a showcase of athletics, rooted
in military preparedness. They were competitions that exhibited
the skills of good, valiant warriors. Troops weren't transported by
jet or a convoy of trucks; they ran and marched. They did not
have modern weapons of war, seeing bombs dropped from the sky,
missiles shot from another continent, or rapid-fire machine guns
that mowed down enemies by the dozens. They threw spears, shot
arrows, and threw balls and chains. When those weapons were
exhausted, they engaged the enemy face-to-face in hand-to-hand
combat. The analogy of a race that Paul uses speaks to the serious
nature of the competition in which we are engaged, requiring the
same serious preparation as that of a good athlete and warrior. Paul
is clear that we must have two essential traits in our lives to be able
to live the life of faith that God has for us. They are self-control and
discipline.

Self-Control

The first characteristic of successful preparation is self-control—
that from which we abstain. This is an essential trait of spiritual
training that frequently becomes rooted in self-righteousness and a
judgmental spirit. We abstain from certain things because it develops
in us spiritual focus—a fuller experience and expression of worship.

It allows us to escape the mediocre life often exemplified by an attitude of "I don't care how it affects me or others." God gives us many things in life to enjoy, but He gives restrictions on their use.

In the early 1990s, I attended a conference for campus ministers in which Gordon MacDonald, long-time pastor, author, and speaker, told us some things God gave us but placed boundaries on them. "God gives us vocation, but commanded rest every seventh day. He gives us money, but requires the tithe to be set aside for His work. He gives us sex, but restricted it to marriage and even set parameters within marriage."[6] In the same spirit, we receive freedom in Christ, but He calls us to spiritual accountability and responsibility. Self-control accompanies discipline in our preparation.

Discipline

The cousin of self-control is discipline. In contrast to self-control, discipline is not the practice of merely saying no to certain actions that are outside the will of God but saying yes to practicing activities inside the will of God. Just as self-control can lead to a judgmental attitude of looking down on others, exercising discipline can result in a prideful attitude of thinking too highly of ourselves. However, this can be avoided when we realize that discipline is preparation to live out faith in the arena of life. The training we do is to prepare us for the fulfillment of God's call on our lives; it is not the totality of His call for our lives.

Discipline in sports is explained as dedication to becoming the very best we can, no matter the cost. The Christian faith requires no less of us to prepare to achieve spiritual victory. In developing the disciplines of the faith, it's important to realize that just as with preparation for athletic contests, disciplines are practiced to enter into competition; they are not the competition itself. The disciplines

---

[6] Gordon MacDonald, Conference Presentation to Campus Ministers in Nashville, Tennessee. Circa 1992.

we practice in our spiritual lives are not to be an end unto themselves but are rather a preparation for the beginning. It allows us to begin a purposeful spiritual life.

The disciplines of prayer, reading and memorizing Scripture, fasting, reflection, giving, and living a chaste life do not comprise spiritual victory. These are the practices that best equip us to enter into the world's arena, prepared to engage the challenges of this world, confront evil, and proclaim the truth without being disqualified. This is victory. Self-control and discipline prepare us for this spiritual victory. Jesus had plenty to say about living a life marked by these two essential traits of self-control and discipline, including making wise personal choices.

Wise Personal Choices

"Be on your guard, so that your hearts will not be weighted down with dissipation and drunkenness and the worries of life, and that day will not come on you suddenly like a trap" (Luke 21:34).

Another challenge to living the life God has for us is to avoid being reckless with our worldly behavior, including what we allow into our hearts and minds. "Be on your guard" brings the implicit understanding of an ongoing battle. We must be on our guard to defend ourselves from temptation. We will be tempted to become involved in behaviors that are destructive to ourselves, our witness, and the spiritual lives of others. It is imperative that we seek and pray for strength; acknowledging the daily battle as we give our lives to God. Christians who take seriously the call to live the consecrated life must determine to keep their minds from being diverted from the purpose of God in their lives. This begins with what we take into our minds.

Guard Yourself

"Take care what you listen to. By your standard of measure it will be measured to you; and more will be given you besides" (Mark 4:24). "If your hand or your foot causes you to stumble, cut it off and throw it from you; it is better for you to enter life crippled or lame, than to have two hands or two feet and be cast into eternal fire" (Matthew 18:8–9; cf. Mark 9:43–47).

The things we listen to and the activities we participate in are areas where we can practically apply our understanding of discipline and self-control. The first practical application is what we allow to impact the way we think about the world and God's work in it. The teachings, opinions, and viewpoints of others have a tremendous impact on how we view and relate to other people. It is important that we evaluate what we are taught and what we read through the revealed truth of Jesus. Often, we try to fit Jesus into the dominate perspectives and culture of the world, thereby diluting or transforming the gospel. This is the exact opposite of what should happen. The gospel is to be the transforming agent, changing our perspectives and hearts and thereby society.

The second principle is that Jesus desired His disciples to understand the importance of actions as they relate to faith. The call on our lives as Christians is a life of outward expression of the transformation that has taken place inwardly. The life given to God in worship encompasses what we do (hands) and where we go (feet). These commands are a direct application of living a life of worship. Where we go and what we do impacts who we become and is a reflection of who we are. There is no room to live our lives exclusively in our minds and with our speech. Jesus considers our conduct to be such a crucial part of the expression of faith in God that He made it clear that the things to which we dedicate our physical efforts reveal our hearts, and our hearts determine our eternal destination. We must stand ready and willing to stop any pursuit into which our feet lead us or stop any action in which our hands are involved, if they prevent us from living a life dedicated to Christ. What we say, where we go, and what we do reveals our hearts.

Speech and Actions Verify a Changed Heart

"Listen to Me, all of you, and understand: there is nothing outside the man which can defile him if it goes into him; but the things which proceed out of the man are what defile the man" (Mark 7:14–15). "But give that which is within as charity, and then all things are clean for you" (Luke 11:41).

Our speech and actions are the testimony of a changed heart. The way we live and how we express our thoughts and values will publically affirm or discredit the claims we make about Jesus saving us. Our speech and behavior reveal with whom or with what we have spiritual affinity. This is built on the spiritual heritage of biblical history.

The call of the children of Israel was to live a life distinguished and set apart from the social norms and culture that surrounded them. In the Old Covenant, God's people adhered to strict dietary discipline. Some animals were called unclean, but there was not anything inherently evil about the animals that caused God to prohibit their consumption. These prohibitions found in the Law were not the first dietary restrictions to be a part of devotion to God. Adam and Eve were prohibited from eating the fruit of one tree in the garden. Nothing mentioned in Scripture indicated that the fruit of the tree was inherently evil. God just prohibited them from eating it and told them if they did eat from it there would be consequences (Genesis 2:16-17).

The religious leaders of the first century drew the incorrect conclusion—that the physical food one consumed either defiled a person or maintained his or her holiness. In fact, they missed the greater point of the restrictions—to help them be set apart from the pagan world around them and to prepare them to be a blessing to the nations (Genesis 12:2–3). They mistakenly thought that keeping the dietary restrictions was all about them and their standing before God. Instead, it was the practice of obedience in order to prepare them to do God's work. The goal of the restrictions was to strengthen their affinity with God, develop the traits of discipline and self-control, and prepare them for His work of redemption in the world.

When our lives are given to God, they are given from the inside out, in full-heart connection to Him, His will, and His character. The commands of Jesus are not a new weight to bog us down in life, nor are they to be added to the already impossible task of trying to live a perfect life according to the Law. We were saved to a new life of freedom, not bondage to rules. This freedom, however, is discovered by expressing the law of Christ, loving others as He has loved us, in all areas of our lives. This is His gift to us. And our transformation is a gift we give to others.

Observing the commands of Jesus are expressions of the reborn life. We are indeed new creatures in Christ Jesus. No longer are we living a life based on guilt or obligation but in true freedom of worship, freely offering our lives as expressions of the love of Jesus, a love that has redefined the essence of who we are—changed men and women whose lives imbue the essence of God's character, which is love. The food we take in is not nearly as important as the love that is a product of our lives. This lets our spiritual light shine more brightly.

Shine the Light

"Let your light shine before men in such a way that they may see your good works, and glorify your Father who is in heaven" (Matthew 5:16).

When we think of being a shining light, we sometimes act as if it gives us a halo effect, much like we see in paintings of angels. Often, we are tempted to like religious accolades, but our lights are not given to bring attention to ourselves but to light the path to God. The light is indeed made up of our good works, but those good works are to point to the Father. As the Temple of the Holy Spirit, we join Jesus as an ongoing Feast of Tabernacles, with our lights shining forth from our lives. "You are the light of the world. A city set on a hill cannot be hidden; nor does anyone light a lamp and put it under a basket, but on the lampstand, and it gives light to all who are in the house" (Matthew 5:14–15).

One of the litmus tests for knowing if our lights are shining in the right way is if our lives lead others to praise God for what He has done through us, not lead them to praise us. So our good works are always done with the intent of bringing glory to God. And when some react by praising us, as Cornelius worshiped Peter, we follow Peter's example and direct that praise to God. Peter said, "Stand up; I too am just a man" (Acts 10:26). John the Baptist understood this when he said, "He must increase, but I must decrease" (John 3:30). Our light must be used in the correct way. We must shine a light on God, not on our public displays of religion.

Refrain from Pretentious Religion

"Beware of the scribes, who like to walk around in long robes, and love respectful greetings in the market places, and chief seats in the synagogues and places of honor at banquets" (Luke 20:46; cf. Mark 12:38–39). "So when you give to the poor, do not sound a trumpet before you" (Matthew 6:2). "Whenever you fast, do not put on a gloomy face as the hypocrites do, for they neglect their appearance so that they will be noticed by men when they are fasting" (Matthew 6:16). "But you, when you pray, go into your inner room, close your door and pray to your Father who is in secret, and your Father who sees what is done in secret will reward you. And when you are praying, do not use meaningless repetition as the Gentiles do, for they suppose that they will be heard for their many words. So do not be like them; for your Father knows what you need before you ask Him" (Matthew 6:6–8).

In reading these passages of Scripture, we almost get the idea that life around the Temple and in Jerusalem was a whole was a lot like a carnival; The "carny" would say, "Step right up, ladies and gentlemen. Pay homage to the man with the gloomy face as he fasts. We all need to have that kind of devotion in our lives. Listen to the trumpeter, and notice his great sacrifice as he gives to the poor. And those people over there really know how to pray. Listen to their eloquence." The only thing is, there was no carny. People acted as their own carny, drawing attention to themselves.

It sounds absurd—outrageous, even—but many Christians subtly practice pretentious religion today. Some people use social media profiles and posts to brag about how their lives reflect and worship Jesus. Rather than drawing attention to God by personally loving people, they draw attention to their own spirituality by publically showcasing their association with God. Others constantly challenge each other in theological debates, trying to flex and display their spiritual knowledge. Others only speak in "God-talk" in public and throw around words that only believers understand in order to demonstrate their spirituality. All of these practices, among others, divert attention from the ways and will of the Father.

Discipline, self-control, and spiritual commitment are not the prize to be marveled at or the race to be won but rather the personal practices to prepare for the race. Athletes rarely brag about how hard they train in preparing for a race, but they always celebrate victory. We are not to create a fanfare of our spiritual discipline, but we can celebrate the work of salvation that God works in the lives of people through our committed devotion to Him. When we glorify our religious actions meant for communion with God and service to others, we elevate ourselves, rather than humble ourselves to recognize God's purposes and work.

Essentially, whenever Christians use such things as prayer, fasting, and giving in competition with other believers or to publically display their faithfulness and spiritual agility, we rob ourselves of the opportunity to run the race God has laid out for us. We turn personal training and commitment into a frivolous competition among believers, with our own superior discipline as the false prize. We stay in training, not ever entering the race to model and proclaim Christ's message of repentance and belief—never achieving spiritual victory over the work of the Evil One through the careful observance of Jesus's commands. If Christians use the church or religious actions to draw attention to themselves for personal gain, they miss the opportunity to follow Christ as He intended.

God is not primarily concerned about whether we can explain a deep theological concept or whether we can use it to show off our religious sophistication. What He desires is a life that practices, through humility, what we say we believe. We cannot compensate in public zeal for what we lack in spiritual depth. Public displays of religion demonstrate a lack of faith, not a strong faith in God. God does not need us drawing attention to our religious devotion to get His work done. God draws people to Himself through many means, but not our contorted efforts at public displays of religion. The religious devotion He requires is faith in action, bathed in compassion, expressed through love, and proclaimed in the Spirit. God working through us is not to become a religious display but should continually lead us to rejoice in our salvation.

Rejoice in Personal Salvation

"Nevertheless do not rejoice in this, that the spirits are subject to you, but rejoice that your names are recorded in heaven" (Luke 10:20).

We are quick to talk about the answers to prayer that God grants us, miracles He works through us, and the blessings He has given to our family, us, and our churches. We lift up the benefits and blessings that come as result of our relationship with God. One temptation is to take our involvement and leadership in the local church and lift them up as religious accomplishments. In doing all of this, however, we fail to keep at the forefront of our minds the gratitude and thankfulness for the work of salvation in our own lives and the lives of others. Jesus did not accidentally command His followers to rejoice in the truly awesome work of God—the work of redemption. When we rejoice and give gratitude for our salvation and the salvation of others, we acknowledge our primary purpose in living a consecrated life.

Rejoicing reminds us that the work of salvation is the work God prizes most. The greatest work that God does in this world is bringing people into a saving knowledge of Jesus Christ. He told His disciples "he who believes in Me, the works that I do, he will do also; and greater works than these he will do" (John 14:12). The work of redemption is the greater work. When we light the path for others to come to Christ as Savior and Lord—to become disciples— we complete the greater work. We are able to do this consistently because we are becoming who God desires us to become.

CHAPTER 9

WORSHIP THROUGH BECOMING

People are drawn to the arts. The arts are appealing because of the creative work of musicians, actors, sculptors, and other artists. The arts are a beautiful demonstration of passion and creativity wedded together to touch the human soul. Followers of Jesus are in the process of becoming like Him, being re-created to be more like Jesus. The miracle of our spiritual development is that we are transformed from broken beings to become part of the structure of God's cathedral of worship—us as the church.

Cathedrals are magnificent structures. Paintings of biblical scenes grace the ceilings. The architecture is inspiring and timeless. The stained glass windows tell the message of the gospel. We are His cathedral, His temple, becoming a spiritual house of worship (1 Peter 2:5). Our lives become a beautiful expression of passion and the creative work of God that touches other human souls. We become a work of art just as a potter molds a lump of clay into something beautiful and useful (Isaiah 64:8).

Jesus is the present one, present in our lives and presently and actively transforming the lives of those who encounter Him. In

Him, we find the living God revealed. We know the character of God because Jesus was willing to be sent, which was His obedience to the will of the Father. Jesus's will was the direct reflection of the will of God. Jesus came to live with humanity and die for humanity to show God's plan and God's way, in God's love.

The biggest difference between us and Jesus is that Jesus was not conceived in sin. He was not destined to sin and fall short of the glory of God. He was tempted but didn't give in. We, on the other hand, inherited sinful nature, were conceived in sin, and born into sin (Psalm 51:5). As mentioned previously, when Christ dwells in us through His salvation, we must go through a transformation. We become a new creature in Christ Jesus (2 Corinthians 5:17). *Becoming* takes time. Upon accepting Christ, we enter into the process of becoming the image of Jesus to the world.

We are to be transformational creatures, simultaneously being transformed and transforming. God works in us to bring this to fruition in us and in others. The extent of our metamorphosis determines our ability to be a transformational force in the lives of others. When we receive salvation, God starts the process of making us more like His Son. When we become more like Jesus, our witness becomes more authentic. Our lives begin to resonate with God's character. It creates a harmony in our lives that becomes the beautiful music of sanctification—that ongoing, continuous act of being set apart for the purpose of God. This becomes such an identifying outgrowth of our lives that our depth of character is evident to all.

When Paul says we are conformed into the image of Christ, it entails both character and purpose. Our lives are transformed into lives of sacrifice, as expressed through Jesus on the Cross. We become completely broken to our wills and agendas for living, putting the spiritual and physical concerns of others above our own. Jesus, even on the doorstep of death, forgave those responsible for His torment and physical pain (Luke 23:34).

Paul paints a picture of how powerful the grip and change of transformation can be in our lives. In Romans 9:3, we find that Paul has such a heart for his countrymen that he is willing to be accursed and separated from Christ if they would come to faith in Jesus. He was willing to give his eternal life in heaven for the salvation of others. His focus had shifted from his own personal and spiritual needs to the needs of others. Transformation and sanctification change our focus to look outward and minister to others, willing to give up everything we treasure to see people know Jesus.

The transformation that Jesus works in our lives leads us to desire the salvation of humankind. As we become the image of Christ, our focus is reoriented to an outward view of the world and how we relate to it. Paul describes Jesus as one who left a position in heaven to become a bond-servant (Philippians 2). We likewise put aside our status as the adopted children of God to be that same bond-servant to the world and commit everything to God for His redemptive purposes. This process of *becoming* is a struggle.

The Struggle of Becoming

Occasionally, I make the mistake of assuming that being transformed in the image of Christ is automatic and will happen as part of my life, regardless of what I do. Romans 12:2 and Romans 8:28-30 speak to this transformation. Romans 12:2 teaches that we are to refrain from being conformed to the world but are to be transformed by the renewing of our minds by the living God. Change takes place when our entire perception, thought processes, and what we dwell upon are geared and focused upon God and His character and will. Transformation can only take place in a person who admits that his or her mind is corrupt, commits it to God, and desires to change. Romans 8:29 teaches us that this transformation is not of our own planning and lofty thinking. God knew before time existed that we would become followers of Jesus Christ. In that foreknowledge, He had a plan for life—for every Christian's life.

This plan is the same for every believer of every generation. We are predestined to become conformed to the image of the Son of God (Romans 8:29). We were created for good works, made known by living a sacrificial life. Here again, we see that Jesus did not come to merely forgive our sins but reversed the penalty and work of sin. Jesus begins His work early in our lives and never willingly relents or surrenders. When we become who we are called to be in Christ Jesus—that is, disciple makers—it causes us to celebrate the truly amazing work of God in our lives and others' lives. Jesus understood and taught that prayer is essential in this process of transformation.

The Lord's Prayer—A Model for Becoming

"Pray, then, in this way: Our Father who is in heaven, Hallowed be Your name. Your kingdom come. Your will be done, On earth as it is in heaven. Give us this day our daily bread. And forgive us our debts, as we also have forgiven our debtors. And do not lead us into temptation, but deliver us from evil. For Yours is the kingdom and the power and the glory forever. Amen" (Matthew 6:9–13).

The Lord's model prayer gives a fantastic picture of what it takes to bring a transformed life to fruition. First, we acknowledge God as "Our Father" which entails the Hebrew understanding of His character and His authority. Fathers were highly exalted, esteemed, and respected in Hebrew families. This address to God proclaims that He is above all. We praise who He is. We acknowledge and place our lives in submission to Him. His name is hallowed, which means "set apart as holy; to honor and revere."

Second, we invite His kingdom to be realized and recognized in our lives and in our day. The time for God's kingdom to become a reality is *now*. This begins with our lives being lived in such a way that they demonstrate how the citizens of His kingdom relate to God and to others. We desire to see the will of God, as realized in heaven, become a reality in our world. He exists in the fellowship of love and we live in His love. He desires redemption and so should we.

His kingdom will be inhabited by those who receive His redemption from sin, embody that redemption, and express that redemption.

Third, we submit our lives to His will, desiring that His will be a reality in the lives of people, just as it is a reality in heaven. We are to set aside anything in our thinking and actions that prevents God's will from being done on earth. We jettison anything that inhibits His redemptive purposes.

Fourth, we ask for the provision of daily needs to sustain us physically. This petition for Him to provide daily needs is done with confident expectation. We don't beg or act as if He is not already aware of our needs. We ask, with full expectation that He loves and cares for us and wants to provide for us.

Fifth, we ask for spiritual renewal through forgiveness. Forgiveness from God ushers us into a renewed relationship with Him. It allows us to experience the relationship with God that He has always desired to have with humankind. The forgiveness of others aligns us with the ongoing work of God's redemption in the world.

Sixth, we ask for a supernatural intervention to keep us from surrendering to temptation and to keep us from the work of the Evil One. This demonstrates our humility and recognizes our reliance upon God to live as we are called to live—how we should live.

Seventh, we close our prayer, acknowledging the same authority and power with which the prayer began—speaking to the eternity of God's kingdom and power. One of the biggest lessons of the Lord's Prayer is that prayers are not just spoken words but a preparation for God to transform the world by His power. Prayer allows our lives to be lived with the power of God.

CHAPTER 10

WORSHIP IN THE SPIRIT

Life in the Spirit

"So Jesus said to them again, 'Peace be with you; as the Father has sent Me, I also send you.' And when He said this, He breathed on them and said to them, 'Receive the Holy Spirit. If you forgive the sins of any, their sins have been forgiven them; if you retain the sins of any, they have been retained'" (John 20:21–23).

There is no greater demonstration and testimony that Jesus is God's Son than these four words: "Receive the Holy Spirit." This is the testimony that Jesus is the one who gives life—spiritual life. God breathed His Spirit into man at creation, and life was given. Jesus breathed His Spirit into the disciples, the same Spirit that God breathed, and new life was given. Life has always originated with the *ruach*, the Hebrew word for "breath or wind", or in other words, the Spirit of God.

The Holy Spirit that Jesus gives us resurrects, makes alive again, and rebirths the spiritual life originally given to humankind by God. The Holy Spirit extends the work of Jesus in the world because it is the Spirit of Jesus. Man's spirit has been made alive again. Jesus was conceived by the Holy Spirit, lived in the Holy Spirit, and was directed by the Holy Spirit. He then shares that same Spirit with us but not for just our own benefit. There *is* a personal benefit, for this Scripture says, "Peace be with you." However, that is not the end purpose for God's life residing in us. The end purpose is that we go as He came—to forgive. We manifest mercy, compassion, and forgiveness to the people of this world. We are commissioned to the same work that Jesus was sent to do by the Heavenly Father. This is how God's kingdom is realized on earth. The Spirit of God is the reason we are able to live confidently in our calling and purpose, to live a life of forgiveness.

Confidence in the Spirit

"Do not worry about how or what you are to speak in your defense, or what you are to say; for the Holy Spirit will teach you in that very hour what you ought to say" (Luke 12:11–12).

Confidence is important in every aspect of life. Fear makes it impossible to be confident. It robs us of boldness and many times causes us to ignore opportunities for Christian witness and ministry. Fear is a tacit admission that we are trying to live the Christian life by our own strength. If we rely on the Holy Spirit our fear of witnessing and living a godly life gives way to confidence. We are confident because of who lives in us. Confidence based on skills or attributes that have been acquired through faithful living or given by the Holy Spirit is built on a strong foundation. Confidence that is based on the overestimation of our skills, attributes, and/or abilities is unwarranted and dangerous.

This latter type of confidence leads to arrogance that blinds us to the very work that God has called us to perform. Our confidence is strengthened and emboldened because of who is working in us and through us, not by our overinflated egos. The Holy Spirit is at work, and cannot be defeated by any power or obstacle. When we lose perspective of this truth, we open ourselves up to celebrating the wrong things in life. Our confidence comes because of who resides in us, not any human trait, skill, talent, or accomplishment. Just as Jesus was sent to do the will of the Father and accomplish His work, so are we, with the indwelling power of the Holy Spirit.

Power in the Spirit

"Gathering them together, He commanded them not leave Jerusalem, but to wait for what the Father had promised, 'Which' He said, 'you heard of from Me; for John baptized with water, but you will be baptized with the Holy Spirit not many days from now'" (Acts 1:4–5; cf. Luke 24:49).

One of the biggest mistakes Christians make is to dive headlong into the effort of making disciples relying only on our own strength and talents. The work we are called to do cannot be accomplished apart from the power of God. We see talented and well-meaning Christians underestimate the challenge of being lights in the darkness. We fail to wait on guidance and leadership from the Holy Spirit. We step forward with all the right motives and good intentions, but we forget one important thing, one critically important thing; it is God's work we have been enlisted to assist with, it is not our work. Redemption cannot take place outside the power of God. We must step forward in His power, but also in His timing even if it means waiting on Him. Once we learn to rely on the provision of God's Spirit, we will have faith in God's physical provisions.

CHAPTER 11

GOD'S PROVISION IN WORSHIP

Avoid Greed

"Beware, and be on your guard against every form of greed; for not even when one has an abundance does his life consist of his possessions" (Luke 12:15).

Many times, one of the outward signs of success is the accumulation of goods and possessions. The reason greed is spoken against in Scripture is because of what it reveals about our hearts. Greed stems from a severe spiritual flaw in our lives. Greed is the result of a lack of faith that God will provide for us in the future, so we hoard present blessings as a safety net. A life in the Spirit leads us to have confidence in God, His promises, and His provision. There is no stronger evidence of living in the power of the Spirit than to trust that God will provide for us.

He provides for our needs—financially, spiritually, physically, and emotionally—because He is faithful. We demonstrate a living faith in the living God when we are able to trust God's provisions for our daily physical sustenance. Jesus leads us away from the practice of greed. When we trust God with our future security, we are able to place faith in His ongoing provision, not in the material things we possess. We must also realize, however, that God does not merely provide for us but provides for others through our generous lives.

Share God's Provisions

"Give to him who asks of you, and do not turn away from him who wants to borrow from you" (Matthew 5:42; Luke 6:30). "If anyone wants to sue you and take your shirt, let him have your coat also" (Matthew 5:40).

Jesus redefines our perspective of money. We no longer see it as something we possess, but as a resource to bless others. Generosity is a mark of the Christian life. It is the polar opposite of greed and demonstrates great faith in God. When we are generous we give evidence of a strong faith in God and that He will continue to provide for us. One of the ways we learn to be generous to others is to learn to give generously to God's work.

When I was about eight years old our parents started giving the three of us kids twenty-five cents allowance each week. That doesn't sound like a lot of money today, but I could buy two packs of baseball cards containing ten cards per pack and have a nickel left over, if I bought the packs of baseball cards separately to avoid the sales tax. So in today's money, with baseball cards as the standard, a quarter would be worth about five to six dollars.

Our parents sat down with us and taught us how to figure out how much offering to give on Sunday morning. They told us that God wants us to tithe, or give ten percent, to the church. The problem: ten percent of twenty-five was two and a half cents. The big question was, do we round down and give two cents or round up and give three cents? My brother and sister chose three cents. I chose two cents.

The next Sunday we put our offering in individual envelopes and placed them in the offering plate. That night dad gave us our next allowance. He gave my brother and sister the same twenty-five cents.

He gave me two dimes. I looked up at him and asked, "Where's my other nickel?" He said, "God loves a cheerful giver, not a stingy giver." I put three cents in the offering the next Sunday. And I got twenty-five cents from then on. I certainly wasn't giving with the right motives at age eight, but the experience did get across to me that generous giving is an important part of our Christian lives. This generous giving is not just to the church, but to those in need as well.

God Provides Our Needs

"For this reason I say to you, do not be worried about your life, as to what you will eat or what you will drink, nor for your body, as to what you will put on. Is not life more than food, and the body more than clothing?" (Matthew 6:25).

This is one of the most straightforward commands of Jesus. Don't worry about the essential needs in life. Worry will only sap our spiritual strength and divert our attention away from the physical and spiritual needs of others, all because we are too consumed by our worries. God provides our needs, most of the time through our hard work and sometimes by unexpected monetary blessings. We are under His watchful care and provision.

Jesus teaches that our lives are no longer focused on our physical needs or how we adorn our body. They are defined by our relationships—with God and people. When freed from worry, we can face life with boldness.

CHAPTER 12

WORSHIP WITH BOLDNESS

"Do not fear those who kill the body but are unable to kill the soul; but rather fear Him who is able to destroy both soul and body in hell" (Matthew 10:28).

Persecution is another threat to the work of God by His servants. Jesus is referring to people who will stop at nothing to thwart the work of God. They are terrified that Jesus will change the culture and political structure from which they find success and change the focus of the people under their influence. They are completely dedicated to maintaining power structures that promote a secular worldview or another construct of faith. Jesus commands His followers not to fear them. No matter the threat, even death, we are not to fear them because our lives are eternally secured because of our faith and commitment to follow Jesus.

Note that Jesus made His disciples aware of the threats and what His followers would face. Christians must count the cost of following God and strengthen their faith, rather than underestimate the challenges and turn away and give up when persecutions arise. We take account for and beware of evil people seeking to destroy us, both spiritually and physically, but we are to remain confident and not fret about the outcome.

Remain Confident

"Do not let your heart be troubled; believe in God, believe also in Me" (John 14:1).

Christ spoke this passage of Scripture with His immanent scourging and death at hand. Additionally, He knew the disciples were about to be tested by people who had the authority to place them in prison and kill them. Christ assured them it was not their time to endure such persecution, but that would come later. However, Jesus gave them encouragement to keep their faith. He also instructed them to not let circumstances, about which they had no control, cause them to despair. Jesus was letting them know that the persecution they were about to witness and experience was not the final chapter, just as the trials and persecution that Christians face today are not the final chapter. Jesus will be the final author who will pen the victory of each individual believer who places faith in Him. For this reason, believers in every century and every locale can respond with confidence, no matter the circumstances we face.

Rejoice When Persecuted

"Rejoice and be glad, for your reward in heaven is great; for in the same way they persecuted the prophets who were before you" (Matthew 5:12).

Christians who face persecution are counted among the giants of the Faith. Our persecution demonstrates an affinity with the great people of faith in Church and Jewish history. The legacy of trials and persecution enjoins us to the redemptive work that God has accomplished for millennia. Christians who endure the evil perpetrated by those who are opposed to the work of God will receive a magnificent reward in heaven. The important thing to remember is that persecution, although terrible, is only temporary. Persecutors will receive a permanent punishment unless they repent, as the apostle Paul repented of his persecution of Christians, and follow Christ. Satan has been and always will be at work to destroy the redemptive witness and work of God's people.

Satan is a transformer as well. He changes people. Evil knows no neutral ground. It only knows victory and defeat in its battle for each human. Satan never gives up. If we embrace sin, it leads us to develop a mind focused on the things of this world. Scripture teaches that Satan is the Father of Lies—the great deceiver (John 8:44). Sin becomes a downward spiral of deception, convincing us that sin is the best life has to offer. We come to believe that our natural desires and their fulfillment are the pinnacle of human experience. But the psalmist tells us the best desires are born from a heart that has an affinity with God (Psalm 37:4). This way of living is completely opposite of following our natural desires; our natural inclination is not to delight ourselves in God or the things of God. Only by God's self-disclosure and His revelation do we see the beauty that is the Lord, His creation, and His work. This revelation creates the avenue to delight ourselves in God, allowing transformation to begin and complete its work in our lives.

The person who follows Jesus will be falsely accused of having wrong intentions or of having impure motives. False accusers assailed Christ, and He told His followers to expect the same treatment. Some people will accuse Christians of being narrow-minded and hateful because the proclamation that salvation can be found only in Jesus runs counter to accepted social and political norms.

Matthew 10:25–26 says, "If they have called the head of the house Beelzebul, how much more will they malign the members of his household! Therefore do not fear them, for there is nothing concealed that will not be revealed, or hidden that will not be known." We are assured that God will reveal the hearts and true intentions of all people. Our response to persecution is to become bolder in our witness. Jesus says, "What I tell you in the darkness, speak in the light; and what you hear whispered in your ear, proclaim upon the housetops" (Matthew 10:27).

Christians often long to be accepted by a certain group of people, which leads us to develop a habit of not rocking the boat. Sometimes this is expressed by participating in behaviors or stating opinions that make us look like we are "with it," socially or culturally. We negate the work of God through our lives because we choose to blend in with the culture, instead of being prophetic. Our response should be to move forward with boldness in the power of the Holy Spirit. One of the marks of living in the Spirit is that our personalities mature. No longer do we rely on the excuse of being introverted, or depend on being extroverted as we confront the demands of living a consecrated life. We are aware of our tendencies but push ourselves, rather we are led, out of our comfort zones to witness and minister to people with whom we are not naturally comfortable. Jesus calls us to be bold, but we should not confuse boldness with naïveté and lack of wisdom.

Be Wise about Outward Threats

"Beware of the false prophets, who come to you in sheep's clothing, but inwardly are ravenous wolves" (Matthew 7:15). "See to it that no one misleads you. Many will come in My name, saying, 'I am He!' And will mislead many" (Mark 13:5–7). "They will say to you, 'Look there! Look here!' Do not go away, and do not run after them" (Luke 17:23; cf. 21:8–9).

One of the threats against the work of God in our lives is the competition from false teachers who mislead us. We battle enemies that confront us, head on and face-to-face, but we also engage foes who infiltrate the work that has already been accomplished. They sow discord and untruth. These foes are sneaky and dangerous. Oftentimes, they display outward appearances of kindness and mercy, but the motive is to destroy the work of God in people's lives by sowing seeds of doubt and raising questions about the truth of the gospel—efforts to undermine His dedicated and committed disciples.

So how do we distinguish between the teachers of truth and false teachers? The mark of teachers of truth is that they proclaim the basic tenets of the gospel, hold to the uniqueness of Christ, and invite others to come to the Light of Jesus. They also model the character of Jesus in their own lives. The mark of imposters is that they begin teaching a theology and doctrine that merely condones and reinforces common cultural beliefs and practices. They explain away the miraculous and urge Christians to ignore the exclusive claims of the gospel. They downplay the uniqueness of Jesus Christ and attempt to bring people together by proclaiming that all views of God and salvation are equally valid. They are often eloquent and winsome, but following their false teachings will lead to spiritual famine.

Beware of False Teachings

"Watch out and beware of the leaven of the Pharisees and Sadducees" (Matthew 16:6; cf. Mark 8:15; Luke 12:1).

The leaven of the Pharisees is hypocrisy (Luke 12:1). The leaven of the Pharisees is alive and well today. Put simply, the Pharisees taught a seemingly biblical worldview, using two criteria to determine who was spiritual and close to God. As mentioned previously, one false criterion was to determine spirituality based on the possessions and the wealth that people accumulated, regardless of how they lived. Another false criterion was the belief that religious heritage guaranteed salvation and favor by God. We see both practices at work in modern society. We may be able to use wealth to buy our way into influence in a local church or rely on our family to assume a coveted position of leadership, but neither will gain us any special favor with God.

The use of the word *leaven* communicates that false teachings have the ability to affect an entire community of people because the teachings are seductive. Once something has been leavened, it cannot become unleavened. These people and those who prop up their worldview through seemingly biblical teachings are dangerous to people's salvation and the advancement of the gospel.

Jesus is warning His disciples to understand the implications and dangers if a person rejects the gospel in favor of these false teachings. It will lead to the same arrogance and hard-heartedness the Pharisees demonstrated. They became emboldened in their false conclusions and teachings, which prevented them from experiencing the very God they claimed to serve. Their continued hypocrisy closed their heart to the work of God. A person's only hope who has embraced false teachings and doctrines is to encounter Jesus Christ and have his or her mind renewed, which allows the person to hear and see God's message of redemption. This leads us to experience abundant worship.

PART 4

ABUNDANT
WORSHIP

CHAPTER 13

WORSHIP IN HOPE

Hope is in short supply in this world. Many, if not most, decisions in life are made from a reservoir of fear. Many of us are fearful of what our children might be exposed to at school, fearful of the direction of our culture, or fearful of the future and what it holds. Fear keeps us from seeing what God is accomplishing. We are assured of one thing: God will work His long-term plan, even if we don't fully understand what He is doing.

Jesus Draws People to Salvation

"Behold I say to you, lift up your eyes and look on the fields, that they are white for harvest" (John 4:35).

The setting of this command must have been unbelievable. Folks rushed to see if Jesus was the Messiah. They came to Jesus because He saw possibilities in a Samaritan woman whose life had been changed by Jesus. Jesus's instruction to the disciples was to notice the people as they made their way to Him to see if He was the Messiah.

Jesus was making a statement through His ministry. He had just had a conversation with Nicodemus, a religious leader, about being born again. Jesus's next conversation about salvation was with a Samaritan woman. Following the Samaritan woman was the healing of the Nobleman's son and the crippled man at the pool of Bethesda. The Christian at worship sees the needs and potential in people simultaneously. This demonstrates that the gospel is for everyone who believes. His love is available to all people.

The Christian message has, at its core, a concern for people. Christianity's message is unique among every other faith in that God initiates love to and for us; we respond to it through our lives. The living God made known in the person of Jesus Christ has people as His first priority—all people. This concern and love for people supersedes any structure, system, tradition, prejudice, or construct of faith.

In this account of the Samaritan woman, some people believed in Jesus because the woman's testimony convinced them to consider Jesus as the Messiah. "From that city many of the Samaritans believed in Him because of the word of the woman who testified, 'He told me all the things that I have done'" (John 4:39). But there were others who believed in Jesus because they heard the words of Jesus over the span of two days, which is confirmed in John 4:41 which states, "Many more believed because of His word." These two descriptions of how people come to believe in Jesus are instructive. Some believe because of our testimonies, and others believe because of hearing the teachings of Jesus. Eventually, however, everyone bases their faith on what Jesus has said and done. The people who initially came to believe in Jesus because of the testimony of the Samaritan woman eventually said, "It is no longer because of what you said that we believe, for we have heard for ourselves and know that this One is indeed the Savior of the world" (John 4:42).

This is a crucial principle to grasp as we live a life of worship in Jesus's name. Our lives are lived in order to see as many people as possible come to faith in Jesus. First, our changed lives are to be credible, and they matter as a persuasive tool to bring others to Jesus. Second, Jesus can still teach others with His words through our faithful teaching and mentoring. Third, as people come to know Jesus's teachings the foundation for their faith changes from our testimonies to Him. We desire to see this transition and growth in the ones we disciple.

God Works Across Christian Affiliations

"Do not hinder him, for there is no one who will perform a miracle in My name, and be able soon afterward to speak evil of Me. For he who is not against us is for us" (Mark 9:39–41; cf. Luke 9:50).

Jesus was speaking to His disciples concerning their efforts to stop someone from doing miracles in Jesus's name because the person was not in their group. This command speaks to our attitudes concerning other Christians who are doing ministry in Jesus's name but are not a part of our denomination. It also speaks about those Christians who are not a part of any denomination. The disciples were dedicated to doing the work of the Lord, but they were more concerned about affiliation, while Jesus was more concerned about God's work being done. Not only is salvation available to all people, the work of redemption is for all people who believe in Jesus. People may not agree on every detail of doctrine that we do, or they may not do ministry the same way that we do, but their work builds up the kingdom of Christ, if done in the character of Jesus.

Facilitate and Respect Worship

"Take these things away; stop making My Father's house a place of business" (John 2:16).

One of the most detrimental actions believers can do is to make the churches where we gather for worship resemble a business enterprise, where some are "preferred customers" and the others are "everybody else." The context of this command is that men were selling animals to be sacrificed. This was their livelihood. They had set up their businesses in the Court of the Gentiles and Women, which prevented access to worship by a huge number of people. Jesus wanted to be clear about this practice: it has no place in God's work of redemption.

Our churches shouldn't proclaim that all people are loved by Jesus, inviting them to accept Jesus as Savior but then deny them full access to worship as God intends them to worship. Every redeemed person is called to live a life of worship and has a place in God's kingdom of priests. 1 Peter 2:5 states, "You also, as living stones, are being built up as a spiritual house for a holy priesthood, to offer up spiritual sacrifices acceptable to God through Jesus Christ." The religious culture of our churches may be the biggest barrier to people coming to know and worship God. The only thing required of all people to find grace and fellowship in Christ is that they repent, believe, and follow Him, thus being adopted children of God— priests of God. They find salvation in the power of the resurrection and live in hope of the coming resurrection.

Hope of the Resurrection

"Do not marvel at this; for an hour is coming, in which all who are in the tombs will hear His voice, and will come forth" (John 5:28–29).

Jesus is telling His disciples to expect to see God at work. Those who believe in the God who sent Jesus will find themselves changed from spiritual death to life. This is evidence of the power of God. No longer will the signs be manna from heaven, fire coming down and consuming altars, or the parting of seas and rivers; the power of God will be demonstrated through changed lives.

The demonstration of our changed lives brought about by salvation will culminate in the ultimate demonstration of God's power—the resurrection of the dead. He who renews our spirits will someday resurrect our bodies. Christ's love ensures that we get to fellowship with Him forever because of the resurrection.

Be Ready

"Be dressed in readiness, and keep your lamps lit" (Luke 12:35). "Therefore be on the alert, for you do not know which day your Lord is coming" (Matthew 24:42, cf. 25:13).

When we are joined with God in this redemptive enterprise, we stay clothed in readiness, our light shining before men and God. This readiness is not an interruption. It is not reading the tea leaves of biblical prophecy and withdrawing to get ready for the return of Jesus. Dressed in readiness can only be accomplished by a life lived in the purpose and call of Jesus as He lives in and through us. The readiness comes through the ongoing ministry of our lives—our righteousness. We are focused on the harvest of people's lives into the kingdom of God. We stay constantly ready because we do not know when He will return.

When we align our hearts with the living God, the God who desires our life of worship, we become focused in our efforts to be a part of God's redemptive work. This is our dedicated worship and it should be fervent, sincere, and urgent, ready for Jesus to return at any moment. Dedication will not cause Jesus to return any sooner, and it should not be used to impress others. Instead, it is the natural expression and mind-set of desiring that life's chorus of worship be enjoined by as many people as possible.

CHAPTER 14

WORSHIP IN FAITH

"Take nothing for your journey, neither a staff, nor a bag, nor bread, nor money" (Luke 9: 3; cf. 10:4). "But now, whoever has a money belt is to take it along, likewise also a bag, and whoever has no sword is to sell his coat and buy one" (Luke 22:36).

The above Scriptures seem to be two contradictory commands to Jesus's disciples. The easy thing to do is to dismiss them as only applying to the disciples who were alive during Jesus's earthly ministry. There is, however, a crucial insight into following Jesus by examining the context of each of these commands.

The first instruction about taking nothing with them was spoken just prior to Jesus's sending seventy disciples out in pairs. It was not a completely risk-free endeavor. Christ even acknowledged He was sending them "out as lambs in the midst of wolves" (Luke 10: 3). The important thing to realize is that they were being sent into cities where Christ planned to visit later, not to the entire world. These cities were filled with Israelites who had grown up expecting the Messiah. Many would have gladly embraced and shown hospitality to people who claimed to be sent by the Messiah and who told them the Messiah would soon visit.

By contrast, in Luke 22, Jesus was preparing the disciples to go into all the world, a largely pagan, polytheistic world. They would proclaim that Jesus was the only Son of the only God. It would threaten the security of many people, including religious and political leaders. In this context, He told them to take money and to purchase a sword, presumably for self-defense. In these two separate commands, we find differing levels of risk and preparation associated with following Jesus and His command to make disciples. The apostle Paul understood this. Sometimes, he embraced imprisonment, and other times, he snuck out of town in a basket by being lowered through the city wall (Acts 9:25). At times, Jesus confronted His accusers, exchanging verbal volleys with them. On other occasions, He slipped through the crowd so He wouldn't be seized (Luke 4:30; John 8:59).

There are two common extremes when confronting risk. One is an aloof presence, totally unaware of the dangers and challenges of our surroundings. This is a naïve approach to the world. This mind-set chooses to ignore the threats to life and limb. It is often robed in spiritual clichés, such as "God protects His children," or "If it's my time to go, it's my time to go." The other extreme is to be cynical and fearful of the world. This is expressed through assuming the worst in people and never trusting their motives. This mind-set frequently sees calamity in every situation.

Jesus was fully aware of the dangers and threats that prevented men and women from following Him. There were outward threats, such as political leaders, and threats from within, such as fear, false teachings, and wrong thinking. One of the dangers of offering our lives without being grounded in Christ is that we develop a confidence in ourselves that is reckless and not from God. When we devote our lives to following Jesus's commands, we maintain wisdom through humility in our freedom in Christ. Jesus prepared His disciples for their ministry, and this preparation included instructions on what obstacles and enemies they would encounter.

Jesus understood the risk inherent in being His disciple, a risk that is still real today. This requires discernment.

Discern the Risk

"Behold, I send you out as sheep in the midst of wolves; so be shrewd as serpents and innocent as lambs" (Matthew 10:16).

Naïveté is not faith. The dangers of the Christian walk are real and serious. Enemies attack believers intellectually, through subtle temptations, outright threats, ridicule, and sometimes through laws or bureaucratic policies. Christians need to be aware of the threats but maintain a life of love. In 1 Corinthians 16:8–9, Paul said, "But I will remain in Ephesus until Pentecost; for a wide door for effective service has opened to me, and there are many adversaries." Acknowledging the power and forces of evil and its enforcers is not a lack of faith. Instead, in spite of the dangers, we demonstrate faith by placing our lives in the most secure place in the universe—in the hand of God. Being in the hand of God does not protect us from death or injury, necessarily. It is a testimony that we live our Christian lives in the power and will of God, aware of the dangers but focused on the opportunities for the redemptive purposes of God.

We commit our lives to God, but we are not reckless, ignoring threats. We move forward under the leadership of the Holy Spirit with wisdom, confidence, and love prepared for the context and culture in which we are sent to minister. We are to be bold but wise. Throughout Jesus's ministry, He did the will of His Father, enduring danger, ridicule, and insults.

Ignore Insults

"But I say to you, do not resist an evil person; but whoever slaps you on your right cheek, turn the other to him also" (Matthew. 5:39).

Jesus commanded His followers to turn the other cheek. There are two important things to understand regarding this commandment.

First, slapping someone on the cheek was a form of personal insult. Peter tells Christians not to return "evil for evil or insult for insult, but giving a blessing instead" (1 Peter 3:9). Paul says, "Never pay back evil for evil to anyone" (Romans 12:17).

Second, people in the Near East, even to this day, kiss one another on the cheek as a greeting and sign of relationship with each other. So the command means we always keep open the possibility of relationship with people who insult us. We turn the other cheek, not to get slapped again—although that is a risk—but to offer the opportunity of a restorative kiss. In doing this, we practice unconditional love—expecting God to work in their lives.

This command is not a foundation for passivism. Christians do have the responsibility to defend themselves as mentioned earlier in this chapter. Also, the Christian has a responsibility to stand against evil and take up the cause for justice. When we see the poor being ignored, people being exploited, people robbed of opportunities because of prejudice, and children being neglected, it is our responsibility to see justice done. Christ was angered at the money changers in the Temple for taking advantage of people trying to worship. Jesus did something about it and it was a physical demonstration of disgust. When we see injustice it should anger us as well. The "Christ love" compels us to prevent evil when it affects or endangers people around us. This is an important expression of love.

CHAPTER 15

WORSHIP THROUGH LOVE

"While they were eating, Jesus took some bread, and after a blessing, He broke it and gave it to the disciples, and said, 'Take, eat; this is My body.' And when He had taken a cup and given thanks, He gave it to them, saying, 'Drink from it, all of you'" (Matthew 26:26–27). "And when He had taken some bread and given thanks, He broke it and gave it to them, saying, 'This is My body which is given for you; do this in remembrance of Me.' And in the same way He took the cup after they had eaten, saying, 'This cup which is poured out for you is the new covenant in My blood'" (Luke 22:19–20).

The Lord's Supper is one of the greatest expressions of worship because it is the ongoing observance of identifying ourselves with the Cross by the symbolic consumption of Jesus's sacrifice into our bodies. We remember and commemorate the total and complete sacrifice Jesus gave for our salvation, and at the same time, His sacrifice becomes a part of our lives. It is the tangible reminder and recommitment to live in the New Covenant—a covenant of sacrifice established by Jesus.

Jesus was broken and poured out as an offering to the world because of God's love for people. The New Covenant calls us to follow Christ's humble example by offering our lives as a daily sacrifice of worship to the world as well, sacrificing anything and everything, if necessary, to demonstrate God's love. Jesus fulfilled the will of God, demonstrating God's abundant love to the world. God's greatest expression of love is the giving of His Son as a sacrifice for our sins. The Lord's Supper is a testimony that we are fully identified with God's sacrifice of love. At all times, we worship in the sacrifice of Christ.

Worship Expresses Love

The essence of worship is the expression of love. As God re-creates the character of our hearts, our love for God flows from a transformed reference point as well. The original command to love the Lord God with all your heart, soul, and mind is wrongly interpreted by some as God instructing us to muster all the human strength, through all the human will, with all the human understanding, by all the human spirit possible to express our love to and for God. This mind-set is not sustainable in living the life we have been called to live. Jesus must change us first.

Now, in the New Covenant, it has been declared that we demonstrate love for God through showing love and kindness to others by meeting their physical and spiritual needs because of the work He does in our lives. We must proclaim that our salvation does not come through our works but through His work. Expressing love like this is not added to our already busy lives, forcing us further into exhaustion and weariness of doing good deeds. This love is to come from a heart that knows Jesus's love, has been changed by His love, and overflows with His love. When our motivation comes from any other place we fall into a performance-based Christianity, laden with guilt and doubt, wondering whether we are doing enough.

The beauty of the incarnation is that the two commandments that summed up the Law and prophets became intertwined with one another. Jesus fully revealed God's love to the world by loving the world fully. Therefore, it is impossible to speak of love for God without demonstrating love for others—the depth of love Jesus showed the world through His sacrifice. He sacrificed His life and His status in heaven on the Cross (Philippians 2:5–8). In other words, our sacrifices should reflect both how Jesus lived and how He died. This becomes our call. To live—and, if need be, to die—as an expression of worship to the living God.

Offering our lives to God cannot be limited to the easy roles or to what comes naturally. God calls for our lives in their entirety to demonstrate the love of Jesus. Therefore, love is not just a gift we accept and admire; it becomes the essence of our actions. Loving God authentically moves us beyond loving only the people our culture expects us to love—people who are easy to love. Loving God authentically transforms our hearts to love like God loves. It moves us to love people outside our families and eliminates the precondition that people must also love us to be loved by us. Love is to be continually expressed. It is never idle or apathetic. Our lives offered as worship engage others and build dynamic friendships, extending the love of God. This is challenging. Love like this can only come from unity with God the Father, through the Son, by the presence of the Holy Spirit.

People try to pinpoint the essence of God. Some would say that the essence of God is holiness, others would say the essence of God is Spirit, and still others might say the essence of God is His ability to create. However, the only thing that allows us to know anything about God is His love. Because of God's love for us, we know about His holiness. Because of God's love, we are wed to His Spirit. By God's love, we are deemed His prized creation. The essence of God is love, which is the expression of His holiness, glory and mercy.

Christian theologian Stanley Grenz states that God has always existed in Trinity, three persons existing in the unity of love. Grenz further concludes that the Father and the Son love each other, and their love is expressed through the Spirit.[7] This is seen in the events at Jesus's baptism. When John the Baptist baptized Jesus, the Spirit descended like a dove, and God said, "This is my beloved Son, in whom I am well-pleased" (Matthew 3:17). If not for love, we would know nothing about God but would be able only to make conjectures about Him and be destined to wonder about who He is. Love is how He expresses relationship. Love is how we express relationship with Him.

Commitment to God ushers in intimacy with Him. We get this backwards on occasion. A major misconception in the modern church is that we expect to experience worship exclusively in a church service, hoping it brings intimacy that leads to commitment. It is no wonder the modern church has fallen into this wrong way of thinking about our relationships with God. We reflect the modern approach to love that our society promotes. The culture says we are to impress someone through our charm, money, a good time, or work, to become intimate with that person and then maybe commit later. God's design is exactly opposite of that. We are introduced to God through Jesus Christ because of God's commitment to us through His self-sacrifice. We respond through our commitment to Him. As we serve Him, our connection to Him grows. Our connection to Jesus is demonstrated by keeping His commands.

Love Expressed to Jesus by Keeping His Commands

"If you love Me, you will keep My commandments" (John 14:15).

Jesus's commandments are life-transforming. They are essential to practice in order for us to become who God wants us to be. They are the hub of living a powerful life in Christ—a life of worship. His commands are the essential tools to show that our lives have been changed by God, that we have committed to live a Christ-like

---

[7] Stanley J. Grenz, *Theology for the Community of God* (Grand Rapids: Wm. B. Eerdmans, 2000), 71–72.

life, and that we trust that God will use our lives for His purposes. Observing the commands are the avenue to renew our minds (Romans 12:2). Keeping these commands are the visible offerings of worship that God accepts. Just as important, if not more so, observing these commands is evidence of our love of Jesus. A life that ignores these commands, no matter how devoted to a religion, is a life lived in self-deception and hypocrisy, a life doomed to only talking about God, not one lived in communion with Him.

The commands are the means by which we give testimony of the reconciled and transformed life we teach and testify about. They are to be wedded into our very being, practiced in concert with the living God. For the commands to become what they need to be in life, people must be committed to be involved in the lives of other people, just as Jesus modeled for us.

Love Expressed to Others by Keeping Jesus's Commands

One may ask, "Why place such a huge emphasis on the commands of Jesus? Don't we live by grace?" Keeping the commands of God has always been the intended avenue of extending grace. Some people mistakenly conclude that keeping the Old Testament Law, and subsequently, the New Testament commands is the way to receive salvation and avoid punishment by God. Keeping the commands is intended to be an expression of a heart already connected to and at one with God. The commands are God's way of showing love between people. If we fail to understand that keeping the commands is primarily for the good of others instead of our good, we miss the message of the New Testament—the message of the Bible.

Mark 10:17–31 and Matthew 19:16–19 record a conversation between Jesus and a wealthy man. Jesus was preparing to leave on a journey, and a wealthy man came up to Him and inquired how he could obtain eternal life. Jesus told him that you shall not murder, commit adultery, steal, or bear false witness. Jesus also told him to honor his parents, and love his neighbor as himself. The rich man replied that he had done all these things. Jesus then said, "One thing you lack; go and sell all you possess and give to the poor, and you will have treasure in heaven; and come, follow Me" (Mark 10:21). The man went away saddened.

This command to sell everything and give to the poor is probably one of the biggest stumbling blocks in following Jesus. It possibly keeps some from seriously considering committing their lives to Christ. This command about selling all our possessions seems to make no practical sense. If we Christians sold everything we owned at all times, we would be living in the streets, homeless, and begging for food. Three important principles are in play in these verses that include the following: (1) understand that wealth does not signify a special relationship or a special blessing by God; (2) the command for the wealthy man to give everything to charity is not a call for every Christian to live in poverty; and (3) this command is not primarily about money.

First, keep in mind the common cultural and religious beliefs of that day—people believed that rich folks had an especially close relationship with God and that they had wealth because of special favor by God. When Jesus told the crowd, in Mark 10:24–25, that it would be difficult for the wealthy to enter the kingdom of God, the disciples were amazed and astonished. In Mark 10:26, the disciples, as a whole, inquired, "Then who can be saved?" Jesus said that "all things are possible with God" (Mark 10:27). Jesus was transforming the disciples' misconception about wealth and its correlation with God's blessing and favor.

Jesus taught that there is not an automatic correlation between wealth and a strong relationship with God. So Jesus told the wealthy man that he would have to give up the very thing that society, tradition, and he himself believed signified special status with God to find the true blessing of salvation and following Christ. Wealth does not mean God favors a particular person more than anyone else. In fact, if a person is not generous and insists on holding on to his wealth, in spite of God's guidance, it signifies a distant and dying relationship with God.

Second, this command to sell all possessions is not a commandment requiring every Christian to live in poverty. When Peter reminded Jesus that they had given up everything to follow Him, Jesus replied, "Truly I say to you, there is no one who has left house or brothers or sisters or mother or father or children or farms, for my sake and for the gospel's sake, but that he will receive a hundred times as much now in the present age, houses and brothers and sisters and mothers and children and farms, along with persecutions; and in the age to come, eternal life" (Mark 10:28–30). So there are some people who have worldly possessions because God has rewarded them for the things that they gave up to follow Christ.

Third, the command to the rich man to sell everything was not primarily about money. The command was given to him so that he would realize that he had missed the purpose of the Law. The Law was about others, not himself. The command was used to reveal the rich man's spiritual poverty. Christ's additional requirement to sell everything exposed the rich man's motives in keeping the law—he was keeping the commands for himself. They are to be kept for the good of others.

This subject is addressed in Romans 13:8–10. Paul, while he is giving practical applications on how to be a living sacrifice, states

> "Owe nothing to anyone except to love one another; for he who loves his neighbor has fulfilled the law. For this, 'You shall not commit adultery, You shall not murder, You shall not steal, You shall not covet,' and if there is any other commandment, it is summed up in this saying, 'You shall love your neighbor as yourself.' Love does no wrong to a neighbor; therefore love is the fulfillment of the law."

Breaking God's commands is a selfish act that puts concern for what we want above the well-being of others. So we don't keep the commands to ensure good standing before God. We keep the commands to show our love and Christ's love to others. Our hearts are united with the love of God toward others by keeping His commands.

This puts aside one of the greatest temptations in this concept of offering our lives as worship. We could be dismissive about Scripture and its teaching concerning a sanctified and consecrated life and merely use the concept of a "life of worship" as a catchphrase to excuse any behavior or endeavor in which we are involved. Jesus, however, had a lot to say about how Christians should live their lives as His followers. Loving Christ compels us to want to embody who we are called to be as His followers. It is a demonstration of our commitment and allows us to experience intimacy with the Heavenly Father to the fullest. Living according to His commands and teachings recalibrates our lives so that we fulfill the Great Commission and exhibit a Christian life.

It also helps correct a common misconception about the Ten Commandments. It is commonly understood that the first five commandments deal with our relationship with God and the second five deal with our relationship with people. The problem with this separation is that it becomes easy to segment our lives into our worship of God and our relationship with people. All ten of the commandments deal with our worship of God and our relationships with people. The love of God and love for humanity were never intended to be separated. 1 John 3:17 states, "But whoever has the world's goods, and sees his brother in need and closes his heart against him, how does the love of God abide in him?" Love is proactive.

Proactive Love

"A new commandment I give to you, that you love one another, as I have loved you, that you also love one another" (John 13:34).

With this one commandment, the plumb line became exceedingly clear for the Christian life. Jesus said in Matthew 22:37–40 that the greatest commandment was to "Love the Lord your God with all your heart, and with all your soul, and with all your mind. This is the great and foremost commandment. The second is like it, 'You shall love your neighbor as yourself." It was such a widely understood precept of faith that the lawyer who confronted Christ about correctly following Him stated that the love of God and love of neighbor was the crux of the Law (Luke 10:25–29). Jesus went on to explain who a neighbor was by telling the story of the Good Samaritan. Therefore, the love of neighbor was always connected to and based upon the human's love of God. It was necessary to explain the term *neighbor* because the people of the first century failed to grasp love's inclusive nature.

Jesus made clear what was inferred in Old Testament passages, such as "So show your love to the alien, for you were aliens in the land of Egypt" (Deuteronomy 10:19), and "The stranger who resides with you shall be to you as the native among you, and you shall love him as yourself, for you were aliens in the land of Egypt; I am the Lord your God" (Leviticus 19:34). In these commands, loving the alien and stranger, is based on God's love for the Israelites. Jesus's command to love as He loved makes clear what was implicit in the Old Testament. We are to love our neighbor as Jesus loves us or, in other words, how God loves us—the way God's chosen were always supposed to love.

This commandment to love others as Jesus has loved us is a perfect example of Jesus's statement, "Do not think I came to abolish the Law or the Prophets; I did not come to abolish but to fulfill" (Matthew 5:17). Love for neighbor has always been connected to God's love for us. Jesus makes clear that if we love ourselves enough to accept His grace and love then we are to love others as He has loved us—loving our neighbor by extending grace and love to them.

Neighborly love is to be extended to all people, not merely those who look and act like us, just as Jesus taught in the Parable of the

Good Samaritan. It is certainly noble, and very easy to say that we recognize the inherent worth of every human. However, it is not enough to merely believe in the unique, special, and inherent worth of humanity; we must have the courage to put it into action by loving people. Christ addressed the subject of love on many different levels, and He wanted His followers to understand what loving their neighbors entailed. This essential understanding is the initial sprout that allows God's love to fully bloom in our lives and brings true friendship between Jesus and us.

Friends by Love

"This is My commandment, that you love one another, just as I have loved you. Greater love has no one than this, that one lay down his life for his friends. You are My friends if you do what I command you" (John 15:12–14).

Friends have common values and interests. The outcome of living out a life of merciful Christ-like love for humanity is becoming friends with Christ. Once again, Jesus reiterates our calling to love as He loved us. Our lives, this expression of worship to God through every fiber of our beings, are to be marked by putting aside our self-interests and sacrificing for others. When we do this, we show we have common values and the same interests as Jesus—only made possible by true friendship with Him.

Many times we confuse being friendly with being a friend. Friendship is much more profound than merely being a friendly acquaintance. Many acquaintances greet me in public. Friends will meet with me over a meal. Closer friends come to my home for dinner (and vice versa). Then there are those friends with whom our family goes on vacation or camping. Each level of friendship brings a higher level of investment but also a much higher reward of fellowship and joy. This is true of our relationships with Jesus as well.

Mutual sacrifice brings the highest and deepest form of friendship, those that last a lifetime. We may think of athletic teams we have played on, marching bands, dance troupes, or choirs, among other groups who have trained or practiced and competed together in mutual sacrifice and concerted effort. These life experiences are essential because they give a tangible example of sacrifice, laying aside personal interests for the good of the team.

Perhaps the reason some churches have a difficult time cultivating strong friendships throughout the congregation is that there are not many times of mutual sacrifice, other than sacrificial giving for a building program, which is private and sporadic. One of the reasons mission trips are a great bonding time, where deep friendships are made, is the mutual sacrifice experienced by everyone in the group. Where mission trips fall short is that they are short term. The commitment to make and be a disciple is a continuous call. A church, at its best, is a church that is equipping Christians to make disciples, no matter the cost—through sacrifice. The wonderful thing about living the Christian life with this type of mind-set and calling is that our reward is to be named friends with Jesus because we share His values and ethics. This leads us to express love to others, even our enemies.

Love Your Enemies

"Whoever forces you to go one mile, go with him two" (Matthew 5:41). "But I say to you, love your enemies and pray for those who persecute you" (Matthew 5:44).

Jesus taught many aspects of love, including love of enemies. I must admit that "love your enemies" is a teaching I would rather not have to bother with. It is already challenging enough to be consistent in loving our families, friends, neighbors, and those in need. Broadening the borders of our love to include enemies takes a high level of spiritual maturity, but we must start by understanding to whom Jesus was referring when He said "enemy."

In the first century, the enemies of God and His ways were government, political, and religious leaders. The Roman Empire allowed and sometimes sponsored the persecution of Jews and eventually Christians. This persecution was realized initially through economic and social discrimination and evolved to include physical persecution and even death. Jews and Christians, would not have viewed the enemies of Rome's government as enemies of the Jewish people and the Christian faith. They might have even relished the overthrow of Rome by outside forces. So it is safe to say that Jesus was not thinking of Christians loving the enemies of the state but of loving people who persecuted them because of their connection to Him. The intent behind this teaching is not a call to advocate against war but to show love, peace, and patience to those who personally attack and threaten us because of our commitment to Christ.

For the first-century Jews and Christians who would have heard Jesus's teachings, an enemy was very personal. It would have been someone who represented the Roman Empire and its persecution, and these persecutors lived in the same community. The soldiers in the story of the crucifixion were not brought in from outside Jerusalem. They were not actors who were called in for a special performance. These men were most likely on street corners, living in the community, and were the enforcers of the will of the Roman Empire. In addition, many of the tax collectors were seen as enemies of the Jewish people because they represented the Roman government. They were the initial perpetrators of discrimination and persecution by collecting taxes in unfair ways. Many people, including soldiers, were involved in the persecution of people of faith.

Just as in the first century, the enemies of Christians are in everyday life. They are not enemies because they upset or offend us, because they try to steal military secrets, or because they are in foreign armies. They are enemies because they try to deter spiritual growth and the expansion of the gospel. Increasingly, in some parts of the world, Christians are being killed merely because they believe Jesus is the Son of God.

In the modern world, who are the enemies of God's kingdom? Is it certain segments of Hollywood? Does it include some college professors who are antagonistic to believing students? Could it be an unbelieving boss who blocks advancement in the workplace because of his or her dislike of Christians? Or does it include overly zealous practitioners of other faiths? Are they a few local government officials who try to block the activity of the church and its people, establishing anti-Christian policies to hide behind and cover their inward disdain for the Christian faith? It could include all these people, plus many more.

Anyone who is trying to deter spiritual growth, is involved in the persecution of believers, and who tries to stop the advancement of the gospel by God's people is an enemy to whom Christ would have been referring. We are called and commanded however, to respond with love. The worshiper must understand, embrace, promote, and exemplify love toward the very people who try to negatively impact our faith and thwart its power. "Love your enemies" applies to all these. We are called to do good deeds for them.

Do Good

"But love your enemies, and do good, and lend, expecting nothing in return; and your reward will be great, and you will be the sons of the Most High: for He Himself is kind to ungrateful and evil men. Be merciful, just as your Father is merciful" (Luke 6:35).

Christian love never means simply the absence of hostilities; it's a love that involves action, a determined engagement with people. This may seem too incredible to be taken seriously. Even more taxing, we are to give to them, for what is lending without demand of repayment? How is this possible? How seriously are we to take this admonition? Quite seriously.

Periodically, students will seek my advice on how to handle an atheist professor they have, usually in an English or philosophy class. Invariably, the students want to use the avenue of writing a paper to call out the professor and convince him or her of an error in thinking. We talk through how to do this respectfully and without appearing hateful, but I also challenge the student to do something out of the ordinary. I ask, "Does the professor know you are a believer?" The answer is almost always yes because of a prior class discussion. I then ask the students to consider doing something kind for the professor—bake some cookies or buy a gift card for coffee and include a note thanking the professor for making them stronger thinkers concerning their faith. I also encourage the students to add that if there is ever a way they can be of assistance in the class that they would be honored to serve in that capacity.

We must embrace the power of love. We must believe Jesus when He says it is through love that people will know that we are His followers (John 13:5). It's not a love that is left in wishful thinking or merely trying to get rid of anger toward others; it's a love that actively demonstrates, through initiative and actions, that God is love (1 John 4:8). This is God's will and our purpose in all of life.

One of the recurring themes in the Gospels is that we are named children of God. This is a powerful identification. To be seen as a child of God or child of the Most High is to have God's character. When we model and practice this type of love, we are exhibiting the character of God in our lives. For God's holy love to take root in our lives, our perspective must change about the work of God. We sometimes never understand what God has saved us to do because we never humble ourselves to admit what He saved us from. Romans 5:8 states, "But God demonstrates His own love toward us, in that while we were yet sinners, Christ died for us." Our standard as God's children is to demonstrate His character. Therefore, just as God loved us before we became believers, by doing good to us, we are called to do the same to others.

The Golden Rule

"Treat others the same way you want them to treat you" (Luke 6:31; cf. Matthew 7:12).

Doing good deeds are at the heart of God's expectations for spiritual living, but the love ethic is not limited to doing kind deeds for our neighbors and enemies. Sacrificial love expresses grace and mercy, not merely kindhearted actions. The command to treat others the way we want to be treated is more than being nice to people. Jesus states this command in the context of showing love to our enemies.

It is showing mercy to people who mistreat us. It extends to every aspect of relationship. God's love is not restricted to meeting the same level of love that another person demonstrates to us. It is treating them with the level of love we want to be shown. For instance, all of us want to be treated with grace for the unintentional—and sometimes intentional—mistakes we make. Do we, however, extend grace when we are the recipients of those mistakes from others? Forgiveness is a powerful application of the Golden Rule—a high form of worship.

CHAPTER 16

WORSHIP THROUGH FORGIVENESS

"Do not judge, and you will not be judged; and do not condemn and you will not be condemned; pardon, and you will be pardoned" (Luke 6:37).

Jesus forgives our sin. This is the central message of the gospel, but there is a stipulation to receiving that forgiveness. We must forgive as well. This makes me bristle at first because of my strong belief that salvation is by grace, not works. We assume Jesus is putting forth a transaction-based proposition in this command. Keep in mind that an encounter with Jesus brings a change of heart. Some people want forgiveness from Jesus but on their terms. They want to receive forgiveness but not offer forgiveness to others. Through the stories in the Gospels, however, a heart touched by Jesus is a heart forever changed by Jesus.

Forgiving others demonstrates that we have moved beyond judging and condemning others. Forgiveness is that proactive demonstration that our spirits are in tune with Jesus. Jesus said that He came to save the world, not judge it (John 3:17). We are sent into the world, not to judge the world, but to testify and show people how to find forgiveness through Jesus, as modeled in our own lives.

There are two different ways to relate to the world: as one who is under judgment or as one who is under grace. What we cannot do is to accept grace for ourselves, but demand or celebrate judgment on others. John 3:18 says that the world is already judged, but Jesus offers grace to the world instead because it reflects the mind, character, and heart of God. God judged the world and found it worthy of His punishment, but He decided to extend a pardon, offering us His grace.

The caveat is that a person receiving the pardon must extend that pardon to others through the grace-filled living sacrifice of his or her life. When we forgive others, it is a continual reminder to us—and at the same time, a statement to others—that we are aware that we deserve judgment, not grace. When we judge others, we communicate that whatever they did was a lot worse than what we did or that they are worse individuals than we are and therefore not worthy of God's grace. The judgment of a person's heart is reserved for God alone. He is the one who sees the heart. God forgave, so we are to forgive. Forgiveness is practiced in the context of accountability.

Forgiveness and Accountability

"Be on your guard! If your brother sins, rebuke him; and if he repents, forgive him. And if he sins against you seven times a day, and returns to you seven times, saying, 'I repent,' forgive him" (Luke 17:3–4; cf. Matthew 18:21–22).

Consistent immorality is rebellion against God's grace. It is, in essence, telling God that He is not enough. He is either not enough to heal the pain that seeks healing in temporary thrills and ecstasy, or He is inadequate to supply all our needs. If we choose lifestyles of immorality we convince ourselves that if life is to be truly engaged and enjoyed to the fullest, then fulfillment must be found in worldly pleasures, temporary thrills, or mind-numbing substances, rather than in a relationship with God. When we see someone who is exhibiting this self-destructive behavior the Christian exhibits compassion and seeks to intervene in their lives. When their immorality affects us, Jesus tells us to forgive and keep forgiving.

Forgiveness is not flippant. Some extend a false grace instead of true forgiveness, based on their real desire to live a life of immorality themselves. Forgiveness recognizes the destructiveness, brokenness, and selfishness of sin but seeks to address it, not condone it. When we minister in Jesus's name, we will confront sin and brokenness. We are going to encounter people, some of them professing Christians, who are living lives immersed in worldly behavior and immorality.

But Immorality is not the only type of sin. "Therefore, to one who knows the right thing to do and does not do it, to him it is sin" (James 4:17). So our forgiveness includes the things that people should have done, but failed to do. This is the forgiveness that is required so many times in our families.

Several spiritual traits are at work in the above passage of Scripture. First is the awareness of sin and its power and influence in the life of every believer. One of the surest ways to fall into temptation is to become numb to the power of sin in our own lives. Christians are to always be on guard against their own weakness to sin. When we see sin in the life of a Christian friend, we are to take action, which leads to the second spiritual trait addressed in this passage—accountability. It takes immense love and courage to rebuke a Christian friend. *Rebuke* is "calling to the attention of someone and reprimanding", but it is reprimanding out of love, patience, and a spirit of humility, with the goal of reconciliation.

Humility in Accountability

"You hypocrite, first take the log out of your own eye, and then you will see clearly to take out the speck that is in your brother's eye." (Luke 6:42).

Self-righteousness and immorality sprout from the same spiritual root. Both lead to the same result: sin, division, and brokenness. Self-righteousness is a rebellion against God's grace by refusing to approach God with humility. Self-righteous people take pride in living the lives they have constructed, shining an ever brighter spotlight on their own religious accomplishments, taunting others with their smug attitudes who don't measure up to their standard of righteousness. They might give lip service to being a sinner, but down deep, they believe that most of their sins are trite compared to the truly big sins of others.

When we confront Christians about sin, it should be with humility. This command reminds us of our own tendency to sin. There should never be a time when we confront Christians about their sin where we think we are better than they are. We approach accountability with an awareness of our own humanity and weakness rather than with a spirit of superiority.

This may be one of the most difficult things to practice in our Christian walk because we spend most of our lives comparing ourselves to other people—academically while we attend school, professionally in the workplace, as a parent when we are socializing, and especially in our spiritual walk. This habit of comparing ourselves to others is very dangerous for our spiritual well-being because it takes our focus off God and puts it on competing with people, rather than sacrificing for them. Paul gives insightful instruction to the church in the area of sin and accountability.

Galatians 6:1–5 says,

> Brethren, even if anyone is caught in any trespass, you who are spiritual, restore such a one in a spirit of gentleness; each one looking to yourself, so that you too

will not be tempted. Bear one another's burdens, and
thereby fulfill the law of Christ. For if anyone thinks he
is something when he is nothing, he deceives himself.
But each one must examine his own work, and then he
will have reason for boasting in regard to himself alone,
and not in regard to another. For each one will bear his
own load.

Paul begins by calling those who are mature spiritually to come
to the person's aid. He calls the spiritual ones to aid in restoration.
Paul also gives a warning that each person must realize his or her
own weaknesses in the flesh. This act of accountability is immersed
in humility. Further, we must bear the burden of another's sin. This
call to Christian accountability is a call to get involved with the
difficult work of reconciliation. 2 Corinthians 5:18 states, "Now all
these things are from God, who reconciled us to Himself through
Christ and gave us the ministry of reconciliation." When we hear of
someone in the church who is discovered to be living or participating
in immorality, we seek ways to help that person that are tangible
and personal. We cannot—we must not—abandon him or her by
withdrawing our love and friendship.

Caroline, our oldest daughter, took ballet when she was four
years old. The day came for the spring recital. We arrived at the
recital later than we had wanted and had to sit in the nosebleed
section of the auditorium. My job: video the two short dances. The
video recorder was large and sat on my shoulder. The viewfinder was
a little fuzzy and not reliable.

The girls made their way onto the stage, all dressed in the
same outfit, and all but a couple of them had blonde hair, just like
Caroline. The dance began. I had the camera zoomed in as far
as it would go and was getting some great video of her dancing.
About twenty seconds into the dance, Sheri turned to me and said,
"Wasn't that a beautiful pirouette?"—followed quickly by, "You are
filming the wrong side of the stage. Caroline is on the other side.

I can't believe you can't tell who your daughter is." I did what any self-respecting man would do. I handed her the video recorder and said, "Here; you film it, then." She proceeded to film the next three or four minutes of the recital. I was angry and a little embarrassed.

After we arrived home, Caroline asked if she could watch the recital. Sheri put the VHS tape in the tape player and as she was pushing play, she said, "Dad filmed the wrong girl during the first part of the dance." After about twenty seconds, Sheri continued, "Now this is where I started filming you." We watched a few seconds, and Caroline proclaimed, "Mommy, that's not me either." I couldn't help but chuckle. Actually I laughed. Sheri had filmed the wrong girl during that first dance too. I immediately felt vindicated and victorious because Sheri had messed up just like I had.

This story is indicative of how we relate to others when they sin. We start, many times, by scolding them or judging them. We, in effect, tell them "You failed and if you were more like me you wouldn't make mistakes." This causes them to withdraw from us because of their embarrassment or anger. The person who gets angry and withdraws then sits back and waits for us to make a mistake so he can feel victorious and vindicated. The problem is this type of action and reaction only results in brokenness, not restoration.

If I had been a good husband, a good Christian, and reacted in the spirit of Christ, I would have realized how important the recital was to my wife and daughter. I would not have celebrated Sheri's mistake but would have been grieved that she missed out on something that was important to her, not taking delight in her mistake because it somehow let me off the hook with my mistake.

We don't find our validation in the Christian life by comparing ourselves to another person and secretly telling ourselves, "At least I am as good as him." Our validation comes from that inner peace that knows we are being good and faithful servants of God's grace. Everyone has a faulty viewfinder in life. This viewfinder is more flawed at the beginning of our salvation experience. Accountability requires patience.

The help we give others in the midst of their sin fulfills the law of Christ, loving others as He has loved us. He bore our sins on the Cross. We bear others' sins and consequences with them so they can experience forgiveness and restoration in Jesus. Many times people who get trapped in immorality already feel bad about their sin, they just don't see a way out. We are called to carry their burden of sin to help them find a way out. We are to be their friend, their companion in finding reconciliation. We all need the help of a friend to find restoration.

Paul concludes by saying that each person "will bear his own load." This seems to contradict what Paul said in verse two. Do we bear one another's burdens, or bear our own load? The only way to make sense of this is that we bear one another's sins, but we bear personal responsibility for how we live and the choices we make. We will be held accountable by God for how we live, according to our potential—not according to someone else's potential. Accountability is always with humility. This accountability is to be as private as possible, ensuring the person is restored, not shamed.

Private Confrontation, Not Public Shame

"If your brother sins, go and show him his fault in private; if he listens to you, you have won your brother" (Matthew 18:15–18).

Jesus has already instructed His followers to do good works and pray in private (Matthew 6:2-8). Here, we are instructed to handle matters of sin and personal accountability in private, if possible. One of the reasons this is commanded is so we never lose sight of our own vulnerability to sin. Private confrontation demonstrates righteousness. When Mary became pregnant, Scripture tells us that "Joseph, her husband, being a righteous man and not wanting to disgrace her, planned to send her away secretly" (Matthew 1:19). God entrusted the raising of His Son to a man who modeled righteousness to Mary, similar to what Jesus would someday command to His followers. He has entrusted the people of this world to us to nurture spiritually with the same type of righteousness that Joseph demonstrated. We do not try to shame people for their actions; we seek to help them find restoration.

Restoration: the Goal of Forgiveness

"Tend My lambs … ; Shepherd My sheep … ; Tend My sheep" (John 21:15–17).

Peter boasted at the Last Supper that he would stand by Christ until the end, even die for Him, but he denied Jesus three times, cursing and swearing during the third denial (Matthew 26:35–74). During this post-resurrection encounter, Jesus asked Peter three times if he loved Him. Peter denied Christ three times, and Jesus gave three chances for Peter to express his love to Jesus. However, there is a much more important and beautiful lesson in this story.

When Jesus called Peter to follow Him, He said, "Follow Me, and I will make you fishers of men" (Matthew 4:19). Later, during the transfiguration, Peter made the great confession of faith that Jesus is the Christ, the Son of the living God. Jesus responded that upon that confession, He would build His church (Matthew 16:16–18). Because of the events of Jesus's trial and Peter's abandonment of Christ at His greatest time of need, do you think Peter felt worthy to fish for men? Do you think he felt he was worthy to proclaim the truth of that great confession about who Jesus is? I doubt it. He was probably full of shame and felt like the biggest loser in the world. But here, Christ is asking Peter if he loved Him, and after each response by Peter, Jesus tells him to tend His sheep, shepherd His sheep, and tend His lambs.

So in this seaside dialogue, what stands out to us through this story is that true forgiveness involves restoration of God's purpose and call in peoples' lives. Actually, it goes beyond mere restoration; it becomes a charge that expands their initial call, just as it did with Peter. Jesus's initial call was for Peter to redirect his profession of fishing to fishing for men. Now, Peter was called to nurture, care for, and lead people. He was called to join the divine profession of being a shepherd of people.

This restoration is not just for our lives but for every human who places faith in Jesus Christ, including the individuals who have sinned against us. Adam and Eve were called to tend creation. Through forgiveness, we have once again been called to tend God's creation. Because of the imparting of the Spirit by the crucified Christ, we are to tend the hearts of men and women, sowing the seeds of the gospel in their lives, reclaiming the divine purpose for humanity—living lives of worship through the observance of Christ's commands.

CHAPTER 17

JESUS: OUR MODEL FOR WORSHIP

The Great Commission is the command that gives the context of observing the other commands, in order to make disciples through going, baptizing, and teaching. It is the avenue of our living, breathing sermon—that defining motivation to keep us focused on what the purpose of Jesus's life was all about. He came to make disciples to give all people in all subsequent generations the same chance that the people of Jesus's time had—and that was to find salvation through repentance and belief. We make disciples for the same reason—to continue the legacy of grace. We must take to heart the ministry of Jesus for this to find its fullest expression in our lives. Jesus showed us some key principles that still apply today. He spent time with His disciples, experienced life with them, and did everything for God's purposes.

Fulfilling the Great Commission Takes Time

The Great Commission requires investment of a limited resource: time. Observing Jesus's commands and teaching others to observe them is a life-changing endeavor. They reorder everything about who we are and how we relate to God and one another, especially how we spend our time.

William had strep throat when he was one year old. Sheri picked up the phone to make a doctor's appointment. Before she could dial the number, Victoria, our third daughter, age three, said, "My throat is sore too." Sheri responded, "Okay, I will get you an appointment also, and then I will call and cancel your play date with Rebekah." "I want to go to the doctor and go play with Rebekah," Victoria replied. Sheri explained, "There is not enough time to do both, and besides, if you have strep throat you can't go play anyway." "I want to do both. Mommy, I want to do both," Victoria said as she toddled to her sister's room. A few seconds later, she appeared with a portable clock in her grasp. She handed it to her mom. Sheri asked, "What is this for?" "I'm giving you some more time so we can do both," Victoria proclaimed. If only it were that easy to extend the amount of time we have each day.

Jesus spent three years with His disciples—it takes a lot of time to bring people to an understanding of the change necessary to incorporate the commands in our lives so they become the fruit of our spiritual connection with Jesus. We must spend time with people. It is a sacrifice of a limited resource. We commit to spend time with nonbelievers so they can have an opportunity to come to faith in Jesus as their personal Savior. We spend time with Christians to see them grasp and practice Jesus's commands. Making disciples takes time—a lot more than a few weeks in a classroom. The commands are best demonstrated just as Christ Jesus demonstrated them, by living among and interacting with people.

Experience Life with Them

Frequently, we view present-day evangelism, spiritual development, and discipleship as consisting primarily of varying experiences of proclamation and classroom learning. We almost exclusively present material consisting of persuasive arguments to commit to one or more religious tasks. Christians are inspired to evangelize, to perform benevolent ministries, and to correct social injustice and inequality. Some examples of these didactic efforts to inspire might include (1) a sermon series; (2) weekly Bible studies led by a teacher and then studied more in depth by the learner; (3) Christian conferences; (4) seminaries and institutions of Christian higher education; and (5) focused training to equip a person for a particular commitment that he or she has made to serve a church. We need these avenues of development in our lives, but a key element must be added—spiritual companionship in life.

Christ emphasized an entirely different model of spiritual development in the lives of His disciples that went beyond learning in the synagogue and Temple. He experienced life with them. We see this in many of the gospel stories. Jesus performed His first miracle at a wedding. He accepted dinner invitations, hung out with sinners, attended religious observances at the Temple, and watched kids play games in the street (Matthew 11:16–17). Christ used these common, everyday events to illustrate spiritual truth, mold the character of His disciples, and model the daily observance of His commands. Jesus evangelized, healed, comforted, taught, confronted the Pharisees, and preached in these everyday contexts. And it wasn't always fun or rewarding for Jesus.

Several times in the Gospels, Christ is frustrated and disappointed. He was frustrated because of the disciples' inability to grasp His teachings. He was disappointed by their lack of spiritual commitment in some settings, such as the Garden of Gethsemane. But through all this, Jesus understood that His primary role was character development. This is how Jesus made disciples. This is how Jesus's disciples learned to make other disciples.

When we think of God's people, the church immediately comes to mind. The tragic thing about the modern church, as known in the United States, is many times it is only thought of as a religious organization. It *is* a religious organization but not one that exists primarily to garner financial, emotional, and servant support of its ministries. The ministries should exist to allow people to learn and observe the commands of Jesus in groups, until they are ready to live them confidently as an outgrowth of their transformed lives. Everything should be focused as a church into developing and equipping believers to observe the commands of Jesus, commands we have committed to learn, teach, and model to others. When this happens, Christians will be transformed by the renewing of their minds, becoming ever more eager to fulfill the Great Commission, as individuals and as a church. The church will become the body of Christ that Jesus intended it to be. This is what we are called to do when we commit to follow Christ.

Our lives are in motion, moving forward, intentional and active. This is true of every healthy person and also true of a healthy faith. The believer's life is set apart, or holy in his or her actions and movement, because it is dedicated to moving forward in Christ, giving an authentic picture of what Jesus is like. The word "go" in the Great Commission can be translated "as you go." This is accurate, provided the Christian's life is lived intentionally in dedicated worship to God. It is not accurate if we are fully immersed in our own pursuits, and we only witness if a convenient opportunity happens to come our way. The ultimate goal of the Great Commission is to see people become disciples of Jesus—a conversion that results in a life of worship.

Jesus committed His earthly life to the process of making disciples. He called twelve men, and He tried to get them to encounter the world with the same character, love, and perception that He did. The Great Commission is only possible with the transformative power of God. Without the authority of Jesus, evangelism may be nothing more than a persuasive sales pitch, always looking for the latest prop, gimmick, or plan to "close the deal." Without observing the commands of Jesus, discipleship can become merely an exercise to impart religious disciplines and biblical knowledge. This misses the heart of the Great Commission.

Making disciples is the heart of the Christian call. So much so that Jesus said, "The harvest is plentiful, but the workers are few.

Therefore beseech the Lord of the harvest to send out workers into the harvest" (Matthew 9:37–38). We go, and pray for others to go, because of our love for people. We make disciples because of love. Love is the motivation for following all the commands of Jesus we are told to observe and teach others to observe. We must commit our lives to these commands because it is God's cause. It will take our entire lives—every role and every endeavor committed to this task—to see our lives offered for God's purpose.

God's Purpose

People are saved for God's purpose. God has a unique plan for each of our lives. Those plans include different vocations and various geographical places in which to live. Some people will be single, and some will marry. There will be differing numbers of children in our families. Our children will determine, through some of their activities and interests, who we befriend. Some of us will go to college, and some will enter the workplace immediately upon high school graduation. All of these things will be a part of God's unique plan for each life.

While there are different plans for each of us, however, there is but one purpose that is common to all men and women. Our purpose is to do the will of our Heavenly Father. Jesus was keenly aware of this higher purpose for His life. He desired to do God's will for His life and did it to perfection. Jesus's life was offered to God. This is evident throughout Jesus's life, especially just prior to His crucifixion when He prayed, "Father, if You are willing, remove this cup from Me; yet not My will, but Yours be done" (Luke 22:42). Jesus knew the sacrifice that was demanded of His life. He knew it would be difficult and painful, yet He put aside His will in order to do the will of God. Our lives are to have just one call, given to one purpose, and that is to worship God with the entirety of who we are. We now turn our attention to some avenues of worship that can be expressed in everyday life. It is not an exhaustive discussion, but it will start us on the path to walk as Jesus walked.

CHAPTER 18

EVERYDAY EXPRESSIONS OF WORSHIP

Reorienting our minds to understand and practice the worship of God in spirit and truth requires offering our lives and every role in life as an offering of worship to God—this has been the central focus of this book. One might ask, however, how to practically do this—what does it look like to offer every role in life in its entirety as worship? This chapter will take a brief look at this concept as it relates to some of the common roles we have in life. If the Great Commission is to be fulfilled in its entirety, this becomes an imperative task.

There is some disagreement with how the word *go* is to be interpreted in the Great Commission. Some say it refers to intentionally going to a specific or foreign geographical location, where God has called us to evangelize, or to set aside a consistent time dedicated to witnessing. Others, as mentioned in the previous chapter, interpret the original language to mean "as you go." With this interpretation, the emphasis is to take the witness about Christ with us in our everyday lives, always ready for an opportunity to witness.

There is truth in both of these interpretations. We must be in the geographical location that fulfills God's call on our lives, found when we seek God's will for where He wants us to live. This will require some to leave the familiar and go to another country, state, city, or culture to make disciples. Yet every Christian must be about making disciples "as we go" through the roles with which God blesses us, provided we are intentional. Keep in mind that making disciples involves all three participles in the Great Commission: going, baptizing, and teaching the observance of Christ's commands. In this context and understanding, the roles are committed to God.

Because an *offered* life is specific and unique to each person, as God created each of His children with specific gifts, I will break down broad principles that are applicable to most people, regardless of their specific jobs or talents. I will discuss common activities that a large number of people share, such as being an employer or employee, church involvement, and school involvement and academics. I will also examine worship through everyday tasks, marriage, and parenting. I will conclude with a brief discussion concerning hobbies and rest and relaxation.

Worship Expressed Through Vocation

There may be a temptation in Christian circles to see only those people who are called to vocational ministry as able to offer their jobs as worship to God. This viewpoint is fundamentally flawed. If this were the case, God would have used only the priests in the Old Testament to do His mightiest acts. In fact, He works quite the opposite. God called and set aside common people to do incredible things. Abraham, Moses, Joshua, and David are prime examples of God using ordinary people for His extraordinary purposes. Jesus continued this way of doing things when He chose His disciples. He chose them from common professions, not the priesthood. He, however, did make the church—His people—into a kingdom of priests. Jesus calls and sanctifies the common person so others can come to know Him. We have the opportunity to offer up spiritual sacrifices every day through our jobs.

My first experience with compassion was through my dad's work as a hair stylist. He has always worked hard for the money he earns and is a good manager of it. One night after dinner, he said, "Come on Billy. You are going to the hospital with me. Mr. Strong has leukemia." Dad grabbed his extra set of tools to cut hair with and we drove to the hospital. Mr. Strong's hair had fallen out because of the treatments he had received. My dad had purchased a wig that afternoon and when we got to the hospital he proceeded to put the finishing touches of cutting the hair on that wig to match the hair style Mr. Strong had always worn. Mr. Strong tried to pay my dad for the wig and haircut, but my dad refused to accept payment. Later, on the way home, I asked why he didn't take the money. He said, "Sometimes you do things because it is just the right thing to do as a Christian, not for the money that is in it." My dad modeled for me what worship through a profession looks like.

When I was a teenager, a physician in my church was a dedicated Christian who made a practice of asking patients if they wanted him to pray for them before surgery. In one particular instance, a patient needed emergency surgery, so there was not a chance to pray with her. However, while the nurses were prepping her for surgery, he asked the mother and father of the patient if he could pray with them. They said yes. A couple of weeks later, while my dad was cutting the father's hair, he told my dad the story of the doctor praying with them prior to his daughter's surgery. My dad's customer then said, "I think he might be a real Christian."

Christians see their jobs or vocations as a part of offering up spiritual sacrifices, an act of worship to God. In Colossians 3:23–24, Paul instructs the church, "Whatever you do, do your work heartily, as for the Lord rather than for men, knowing that from the Lord you will receive the reward of the inheritance. It is the Lord Christ whom you serve." I realize this passage of Scripture was written in reference to slaves, but neither I nor this passage condones slavery. There is, however, a direct application as it relates to our everyday jobs—our work is not done for our employers, and if we are the employer, work is not done merely for ourselves. Our work is done for the Lord. We serve the Lord through our jobs.

As long as we are involved in honorable and moral professions, our work serves as an example to our employers, fellow employees, customers, vendors, and the public of our dedication and service to the Lord. Christian employees are to be hard-working, always giving their best and seeking to be productive in the workplace, regardless of how they are paid in comparison to another person. The Christian doesn't work for merely a paycheck but for God, through his or her dedication. In this way, God blesses the employer through the Christian worker, whether the employer recognizes the blessing is from God or not.

In Colossians 4:1, Paul also gives instructions to the employer. "Masters, grant your slaves justice and fairness, knowing that you too have a Master in heaven." Again, I am not condoning slavery, but this passage has a direct application for the work place. Employers and organizational leaders are to never exploit employees and must realize that God has given them the honor and important task of being an employer, leader, and/or supervisor. This important task of leadership in the workplace is the avenue that God has chosen to make sure that employees and their families are provided the food, clothing, and shelter they need. Some Christian employers and organizational leaders fall prey to the great deception that their roles as employers or organizational leaders begin and end with making money or seeing the organization thrive and survive. The greatest role they have is to model the character of Jesus through the way they relate to and lead the people God has made dependent on their God-given gifts of business acumen and leadership.

The Christian businessperson works to earn a profit, and an organizational leader works for the success of the ministry or organization he or she leads. However, the success that comes is not just for the benefit of the bottom line of the business or organization or for the employer or leader; it's for everyone who works in the business or organization and everyone who is served by the business or organization. The practice of this ethic will determine how the employer or leader is judged to be aligned with the character of God.

God is merciful, generous, patient, just, and a great provider, among other character traits. God also expects us to live to the fullest potential of our gifts and abilities with these character traits as well—no matter the setting. The employer or organizational leader is expected to demonstrate the character traits of God in personal interactions, but he or she also has the duty to expect the employees to give their best efforts while at work. This is the employer's responsibility and when done in God's character is a crucial means of teaching accountability. Vocation is the role that encompasses a huge portion of our lives. If we are serious about our lives being offered to God as worship, this part of our lives must be dedicated to the Lord and committed to His purposes. Work and church are not unrelated activities to be lived out in mutual isolation; rather, they are blended by our overarching expressions of worship.

Worship Expressed Through Church Involvement

Church involvement is a crucial part of the life of a Christian. Every Christian should be involved in the ministry of a local church. Lives are changed because of the dedicated service of Christians. There are four people I want to mention briefly who impacted my life through their service in a church. I don't share these things because I think I grew up in the gilded age of the church or because my childhood was perfect. I share them because these people demonstrated a life of worship that serves as an example to us.

The first is Mr. Bill Parrish. He is the first memory I have of someone serving in a church. He would stand at the top of the stairs to the nursery and children's area of Emmanuel Baptist Church and open the door for families so they could drop their pre-school children off for Sunday School. Every Sunday he would smile, rub the top of my head as I walked inside the door and say, "Good to see you today, Billy. Glad you're here." The first time I remember being sad was when he died a few years later. In some ways he is still the face of the church for me. He painted a picture of the church as a friendly, welcoming place. He had what many would consider a small role in the church, but I wonder how many children and their families he influenced.

The second is Mrs. Tapscott. When I was in the fourth grade my parents felt led to move our family to First Baptist Church. I was ushered to the fourth grade Sunday School class. I was walking into a new church, being led to a new class. I wore thick, "Coke bottle bottom" glasses and had silver caps on my two front teeth because I had chipped them playing basketball in the second grade. I was self-conscious about my appearance and really did not like new groups. I remember standing in the doorway of that classroom. All the kids turned and looked at me. I only knew one boy in the room from our previous church. Mrs. Tapscott walked over to us and greeted my dad and me, kneeled down and gave me a big hug and told me she had saved a seat just for me. Her graciousness and welcoming spirit made all the difference that morning. Her kindness throughout that year made a huge impact on my life and taught me to show kindness to everyone regardless of their appearance.

The third is Mr. Ron Pepper. He was our seventh grade Sunday School teacher. Mr. Pepper was a man's man. He was a good athlete, especially in basketball. He must have stood six feet seven inches tall. He was an engineer by profession. One Sunday, the teachers split the class into boys and girls to talk about biblical teachings concerning sex. He taught a very good lesson on the subject and at the conclusion of it he shared from his personal life. Needless to say we were all quiet and tuned in when he was speaking.

He said, "Young men, listen to me. This is an important issue. You are going to have many opportunities in your teenage years to sleep with girls. Two things will happen if you do. First, you will hurt the lives of these girls. Second, you will rob yourself of something very special. My wife, Carol, and I have never slept with anyone else. Our wedding night was the first time either one of us experienced sex. This is an ongoing gift we give to each other. Exercise the self-control now and the reward will be great later." I remember thinking, "So my parents aren't the only ones who believe that." Godly people teaching biblical truths have a tremendous impact on young people and are key to disciple making.

The fourth is Mary Ann Brining. She was one of my high school Sunday School teachers at our church. One Sunday she was teaching on the birth of Jesus and mentioned that Mary was a virgin when she became pregnant with Jesus. I was a little skeptical of the claim as I was concerning a lot of the miracles in the Bible. I approached things almost exclusively from a rational basis at that time in my life. I demanded proof or a logical explanation. I asked her, "Is there any proof Mary was a virgin other that what is written in the Bible. And, if not, how can we know for sure it happened that way?" She didn't panic, nor was she offended by the question. She simply stated, "Billy, there are a lot of things written in the Bible that can't be proven. If they could, there would not be room for what is truly important and that is faith. Some things you just have to accept by faith." I was not impressed with her answer. I had heard that before.

Several years later I was sitting in a seminary theology class and the subject of the virgin birth came up. I had moved past my demand to have proof for everything that was written in Scripture, but I asked the professor the same question I had asked Mrs. Brining. I wondered if there was a better explanation. Dr. Kirkpatrick responded, "Bill, some things you have to accept by faith. We can't demand that God work the way we want Him to work. One of the most difficult things to do is to open our hearts to the way God has chosen to reveal Himself. One of the ways He has chosen to reveal Himself is through the testimony of Scripture. We have to exercise faith to accept His revelation."[8] After hearing that I became a lot more impressed with Mrs. Brining's response.

These people, along with my parents and scores of others in those two churches, were instrumental in my conversion and spiritual development. Church is an important place for disciple making. Each Christian should explore and commit to serving a local congregation. Serving others through the ongoing ministry of the church is an important avenue of worship. We serve a church because it prepares people to make their lives an offering to God.

Worship Expressed Through School Involvement and Academics

Seventeen years of our lives are spent in school if we begin in kindergarten and go through four years of college. During these years we interact with hundreds, sometimes thousands of people. We are involved in clubs, athletics, music groups, ministries, among many other pursuits and interests. In addition to the social aspect of education there is the academic element. Both of these school experiences are crucial in developing and expressing a life of worship.

First the social interaction. Christian students have tremendous opportunities to impact the lives of others with an embodiment of the love of Jesus. One of the challenges in school is that many Christians are drawn to the same thing as non-Christians and that is to be included in a group of students. Whether students are popular, loners, or somewhere in between, every student struggles with acceptance and validation. Pressure for social conformity is palpable and ongoing. This leads to the development of exclusive sets of friends, even at church.

Churches can unwittingly play into the pressure to conform. It is common for church student groups to reflect one of the

---

[8] David Kirkpatrick, Systematic Theology Class at Southwestern Baptist Theological Seminary, Fort Worth, Texas. Spring Semester, 1984.

predominant groupings of students on campus. These divisions are sometimes promoted by the church youth group and its leaders. The challenge of parenting and church leadership is to equip and encourage students to relate across student groupings. Conformity to a group must be replaced with an important character trait of God. He shows no partiality between people but treats people in every social class the same (Acts 10:34–35). A Christian student should strive to count among his or her friends people from different segments of the student body. The biggest barrier to implementing this mindset is fear of loneliness, exclusion, or ridicule.

Parents' and church leaders' first priority is to equip students to stop pursuing inclusion and popularity like moths drawn to a flame, but instead focus their lives on significance. When a student is focused on significance they can take their gaze off of the trap of popularity and acceptance and notice the people who are being shunned from social circles. They notice students whose spirits are downtrodden because of difficult home situations or who are being ridiculed by peers. It will take a spiritually confident and mature student to notice and seize these opportunities, but he or she will make a lasting impression on others' lives. This is worship through school involvement—being an offered student.

Second is the matter of academics. Students have a spiritual responsibility to do the best they can in the classroom. This builds credibility with teachers, professors, and peers. Academic achievement is not just for personal success and preparation for a career, it opens up more avenues through which to worship. The witness of a student to instructors and peers is strengthened by excellence in the classroom. When we are in school, academics is our profession and our school work should be done as if it were being done for the Lord. In addition, excellence in the classroom helps build a strong work ethic, discipline, and self-control, all traits that are essential life skills and important for faith development.

School is a difficult setting in which to worship. Many times, the cultural and social pressures seek to dilute the witness of Christians.

Parents and churches must focus efforts to equip students to live a life committed to observing the commands of Christ in school life.

Worship Expressed Through Everyday Tasks

"I'm going to buy groceries." "I'm going to fill the car up with gas; I'll be back in a few minutes." "I'm taking William to the doctor this morning." Sheri and I say phrases like these many times over the course of a year. Let's face it; life is not always exotic. Life requires everyday tasks and duties to function as it should. Can these common, sometimes mundane tasks be worship? Yes, they can.

I am a type-A personality, especially with tasks and errands. I have walked across campus, mind intent on getting to a meeting with an administrator and never noticed any students as I walked. I can also walk through a parking lot, get a buggy, fill it with groceries, pay for the food, and go home, never engaging anyone in conversation. Worse than that, I used to not even notice anyone around me. I wasn't rude, just in a hurry. I wanted to get to something more important. I was thinking about something more important—or so I thought for years.

Sheri is just the opposite, and I have learned a tremendous amount from her in our marriage. I recall many times, upon returning from the store, she would ask me, "Who did you see at the store?" I would stand there a little dumbfounded, shrug, and say, "No one." Going to a public place with her is total engagement. She calls everyone she knows by name, asks how their children are doing, mentioning a recent accomplishment she read about in the local paper or heard about from someone else. She may inquire about a sick mother or father. She engages the teller and the people behind her in line with smiles and kind words. She is truly amazing.

A couple of years ago, I determined to change in this area of my life. I pulled into a parking space, turned the ignition off, and made a commitment to be engaging and demonstrate the spirit of Jesus. It was not easy, not because I was shy, awkward, or socially backward but because it took focus and energy to connect to the real world around me. My heart has changed in this area of my life. What I realized about myself as I have reflected on all this was that I had similar behaviors when I was doing any task that I didn't look forward to doing. It struck me that most of the people with whom I come into contact during any given week is when I am doing ordinary tasks and errands.

Christians should be the kindest persons that a teller, fast-food worker, receptionist, car mechanic, teacher, or sports coach encounters. Just imagine how many complaints and grumpy attitudes they get during the course of a day. "Love, joy, peace, patience, kindness, goodness, faithfulness, gentleness, and self-control" are the essential fruit of the Spirit in these settings (Galatians 5:22-23). Christians bring the Light of Jesus into everyday life through common tasks, embodying love—this is worship.

Worship Expressed Through Marriage

We have roles that may include being a husband or wife, parent, child, grandparent, or sibling. Each of these roles is to be offered to God. We will look at the roles of spouse and parent for the purposes of this book. A huge part of life for most adults is that of being a husband or wife. The way we relate to our spouses is crucial in committing every aspect of our lives as worship to God. The primary reason God established marriage relationships was for a man and woman to join together to fulfill God's plan. Scripture reveals that Eve was to be a helper with Adam (Genesis 2:20). They were given the same role of stewardship over the earth. They were to work together to care for and enjoy the world God created, as well as enjoy one another (Genesis 1:28).

A good marriage is comprised of a man and woman who have common goals and aspirations. However, the best marriages are partnerships, two people dedicated to seeing the will of God realized in the life of their family and joining together to worship God through their marriage. The state of our marriages affects how we view and relate to everyone in our families and those outside of our families. A Christian husband and wife see their marriage in the context of worship. Paul summarizes his instructions about how a wife and husband should relate to one another by stating, "Nevertheless, each individual among you also is to love his own wife even as himself, and the wife must see to it that she respects her husband" (Ephesians 5:33).

A Christian husband seeks to see the faith of his wife strengthened, and he either affirms or discredits the work of God in his life and in the marriage relationship by the way he loves his wife. A marriage that is insecure in this basic fabric of a husband's commitment to his wife cannot focus outwardly to the world, nor can the husband be involved in credible and meaningful discipleship of his children. Husbands are instructed in Ephesians 5:25 to "love your wives, just as Christ also loved the church and gave Himself up for her." Jesus's love for the church culminated in sacrifice. Therefore, at its heart, this instruction means a husband's relationship with his wife should be marked by sacrifice.

A husband cherishes his wife by putting concern for her above concern for himself. The practice of making disciples parallels a marriage, in that both require intentional investment of time with another person. A husband demonstrates his love for God by connecting with his wife, spiritually and emotionally, in loving her. The husband who is serious about offering his role as a husband as worship to God will refrain from comparing his wife to other women. He only has "eyes" for his wife. He is to be content with and take delight in the precious gift God has given him in his wife. The children in their family will recognize a father who esteems his wife. This selflessness on the part of the husband will give the children an example of the character of Christ and the selflessness He showed the world.

A husband loves his wife by showing appreciation for her investment in the marriage and family. This investment may look different in the various chapters of life and in different families. A wife may be a stay at home mom, businesswoman, minister, educator, or work in a trade, among many other professions. Each couple must determine what God is leading them to do. The husband loves his wife by encouraging her to pursue God's will for her life as a wife and mother in the home and/or as a professional in the workplace, seeing her as a worshiper of God through her God-ordained roles and profession.

A Christian wife also seeks to see the faith of her husband strengthened. A wife either affirms or discredits the work of God in her life and in the marriage relationship by the way she respects her husband. A marriage that is insecure in the basic fabric of a wife's commitment to the marriage cannot focus outwardly to the world, nor can she be involved in credible and meaningful discipleship of her children. The wife will show respect for her husband by not comparing him, his work, or his success with other men. She celebrates by showing respect for her husband as he follows God's will and purpose for his life, submitting her own will in sacrifice to God by partnering with her husband as he champions the cause of God in the family and in the world. He could be a stay-at-home dad, businessman, minister, educator, or work in a trade, among many other professions. The children in their family will recognize a mother who respects her husband by showing him love through respect—her act of submission. This demonstration of respect will instill in their children a respect for the Lord, teaching them valuable lessons in relating to their spouses and to Jesus.

Marriage is also given for the benefit of the man and woman through fulfillment of physical needs. God told Adam and Eve, "Be fruitful and multiply" (Genesis 1:28). Genesis also says, "For this reason a man shall leave his father and his mother, and be joined to his wife; and they shall become one flesh. And the man and his wife were both naked and were not ashamed" (Genesis 2:24–25). Proverbs 5:18–19 says, "And rejoice in the wife of your youth ...

Let her breasts satisfy you at all times; Be exhilarated always with her love."

Sexual intimacy is an important part of marriage. It is a celebration of the creative work of God—His gift to us. Sexual union between a man and woman married to one another recognizes and celebrates the wonderful gift God has given through marriage. Any other sexual union is not blessed by God. A marriage ceremony inaugurates worship in marriage that becomes a continual act of worship to God through love and respect for one another, service to God, and sexual fidelity with one another. This likely will bring children into the family, either through birth or adoption.

Worship Expressed Through Parenting

Christian parenting is a challenge but one of the highest callings a person can have. The primary thing to keep in mind as we parent is that our children are given to us, but they are, first and foremost, God's children. God has entrusted their spiritual growth into our hands. Our job as parents is to challenge, nurture, and guide our children to become the disciples God would have them become. We are to unlock their spiritual potential and strive to bring them to open their hearts to follow God, no matter where He leads them to live or whatever He calls them to do. We are to push our children to engage the people they socialize with at school and church. We are to instill biblical truths and the importance of Scripture as their guides for life.

There is no recipe for bringing this to fruition. Even within the same family, every child is different. All four of our children are unique. Sometimes it is difficult to believe they have the same parents. The most important thing to realize is that personal sacrifice is required to see children grow into the women or men God wants them to be. The two principles of spending time and experiencing life together, discussed previously, are crucial for parents as they raise and disciple their children. There is a misconception that "quality time" is more important than the "quantity of time" we spend with our children. It takes both. But, all of our time is not to be invested with our children.

One of the things that we must model to our children is what a sacrificial life looks like. Parents can sometimes fall into the trap of thinking that every moment they are not working or not at church must be spent with the kids. We should spend time with our children, but we are also to model for them what investing in our community and others' lives looks like. Children should see parents who are sacrificing for people outside of their family.

Parents shouldn't try to do everything, but there should be at least one thing we commit to that helps improve the lives of others whether that is coaching a sports team, leading a scout troop, volunteering for community service, being a chaperone on a school trip, among other avenues of service. The important thing is to communicate with our children why we do these things and talk to them about ways God has used our service. If we just focus on our families, we hamstring our children in their spiritual development. We will have modeled for them a self-centered life and they will have a more difficult time understanding how to fulfill the Great Commission in their own adult lives. A sacrificial life teaches children to be unselfish and models Christian service to them—how Christian worship is embodied in everyday life.

Worship Expressed Through Our Hobbies

My mom is a fabulous seamstress. She sewed a lot of our clothes when we were growing up, as well as the drapes and curtains in our home. She sewed Sheri's wedding dress and has sewn Easter dresses for all six of her granddaughters. Several years ago, my hometown, Moore, Oklahoma, was hit by an F-5 tornado. Plaza Towers Elementary School was destroyed and seven students lost their lives in the storm. It was a heart-breaking and gut-wrenching experience for the families, school, and city. Emmaus Baptist Church, the church my parents attend, opened its doors and let the students attend school there until the elementary school could be rebuilt.

Mom was part of a quilting ministry that made items for various charitable causes as well as for our troops overseas. Because of this ongoing ministry, the school couldn't use that particular room for class one day per week. Mom overheard one of the students tell another student, while explaining why the ladies were sewing, "I think they do it because they love Jesus." Several weeks later some of the students, on their own initiative, asked if they could come in and pray over the quilts.

My dad is an avid outdoorsman. One of the men my dad fished with was Charles Greer. He was a retired mail carrier. One day dad, Mr. Greer, another friend of my dad's, and I went fishing at Lake of the Arbuckles in Southern Oklahoma. I was almost fourteen years old. I went fishing with Mr. Greer in his boat. Later that morning Mr. Greer asked me if I wanted to pilot the boat. I was glad to do it.

He had a small boat with an outboard motor. It was the kind of motor that had hand controlled steering with a throttle on the end of it. We sat facing the rear of the boat as he showed me how to start the motor, throttle the motor in forward and reverse, and steer it. I was set. He made his way to the front of the boat and climbed out so he could push us off the shore. He gave a big shove and jumped into the boat and told me to start the engine and back away from the shore. I did, but something went wrong.

I had learned how to throttle the engine looking at the rear of the boat and when I was facing forward, my arm extended behind me something got crossways in my mind. Instead of throttling the boat in reverse, I throttled it to move forward, and very fast I might add. It lunged forward, going ashore on some loose gravel and Mr. Greer went flying out of the boat and landed face down on the smooth gravel rocks. I was mortified.

He got up, brushed his pants and shirt off and walked to the front of the boat. I had gotten up and jumped out to see if he was ok and said repeatedly how sorry I was. He simply replied, "Now that didn't go as planned. Everything is ok." I said, "I guess you will want to pilot the boat. I will push us off." He stopped and said, "Oh no. Billy you are still going to pilot the boat. You can't give up or walk away from things in life when you make a mistake. You ask forgiveness, learn from it and keep moving forward. Now, let's try this again."

We spent the day fishing, talking about life, sports, girls, school, and faith. Later that afternoon we met up with my dad. I was still piloting the boat. My dad asked how the fishing went. He then asked Mr. Greer about my piloting skills. I ducked my head a little, expecting my mistake to be told to my dad and the other man in the boat with him. Instead, Mr. Greer said, "He is a good pilot. He will be ready to pilot your fancy boat in no time." No mention was made of my mistake. I learned a lot about Jesus that day from Mr. Greer. He taught me, forgave me, was my advocate, and entrusted me with something that was important to him. Whether it is rock climbing, quilting, cooking, fishing, or a sport you love to watch or play, others will be blessed as you carry the Spirit of Christ into that activity. It is a crucial part of a life of worship.

Worship Expressed Through Rest and Recreation

Is there any time to relax and rest? It may seem that this concept of offering ourselves as worship leads to continual work and exhaustion. Instead, it should result in just the opposite. We do work hard, but we refrain from overcommitting so that the roles with which we are entrusted can be offered as the best possible worship. Rest and personal care are essential in our lives of worship. We find this principle at work in the words of Jesus when He said, "The Sabbath was made for man, and not man for the Sabbath" (Mark 2:27). We find a close connection between rest and commitment to God. God rested on the seventh day after He created everything (Genesis 2:2). Every seventh year, the land was to be given rest by not planting anything (Exodus 23:11). In addition, every fifty years, the land was not to be plowed and planted (Leviticus 25:8–55). If the land was given rest from producing food, one could reasonably conclude that the work of servants and landowners would have been greatly scaled back.

Humans need down time. Deuteronomy 5:12–15 commands observance of the Sabbath. The passage teaches that the command is based on God's deliverance from the land of Egypt. So the Sabbath is a celebration of freedom. This down time is not an indicator of a lack of worship, just a different expression of it. Assumed in this view of rest and recreation is that we have been working diligently the other six days.

One day of rest per week, or one seventh of our lives, is a gift from God to give thanks for the blessings He has given through our hard work by resting from that same work. We enjoy the creation He has given us and look forward to the week to come with renewed commitment. The wonderful thing about this rest is that God works in us during this time of rest and recreation to renew us, spiritually and physically. We need some time alone during our rest and relaxation, just as Jesus did. When we offer every role, activity, relationship, and our rest and relaxation to God we begin to experience worship as the ultimate expression of life.

CHAPTER 19

WORSHIP: THE ULTIMATE EXPRESSION OF LIFE

Worship, as described in this book, begins with an experience with the transcendent and immanent God, continues through a companionship with the transcendent and immanent God, and culminates with an eternal relationship with the transcendent and immanent God. Many Christians want to hang on to the initial experience of salvation or focus entirely on heaven. But worship is acting upon the promise of God's salvation intersecting, as He did through Jesus, His creation. Hebrews 11 honors the faith of the men and women of the Old Testament. It was not a faith of speculation about God, but a faith acting on His promises.

The same is true of Christians today. Merely receiving and acknowledging the promises of Jesus is not how faith is lived. Faith is demonstrated by how we live between receiving salvation and receiving the reward in the life to come. Faith is demonstrated by how we stake our lives on the promises and commands of Jesus. It takes a tremendous amount of faith to incorporate the commands of Jesus into our hearts, actions, and roles in life. This gives testimony to our confidence that the observance of Jesus's commands are the superior way to relate to God and people. Becoming His disciple by observing them is a superior way to live. When we live our lives by staking our lives, "our everything," on Jesus, we will stand in true awe of God, a God who is faithful to be immanent—present with us in every situation in life. The life God wants us to live is a faith in action between the starting blocks and the finish line of salvation.

Life Between the Starting Blocks and the Finish Line

Worship is meant to be expressed in the race of the Christian life. Many believers are diverted from the Christian race as they chase after their own pursuits. They veer from God's path, taking their own route, and fall into the temptation of off-roading shortcuts through immoral behavior or self-determined pursuits. In Christian circles, we define sin as falling into immoral behaviors or self-determined pursuits. Sin is running from God and chasing after our own ever-changing desires. This is a serious setback to maintaining a life of worship that requires forgiveness and restoration.

There is, however, a more subtle and equally dangerous action that is all too common for the believer who seemingly has his or her religious life in order. It derails believers, crippling them from the ability to jump over the hurdles in the Christian race. It prevents Christians from ever experiencing the abundant life in Christ Jesus. The temptation is to cling to the starting line or finish line rather than run the race. The temptation is to either keep our focus entirely on our past salvation experiences or stay focused on heaven and never live by faith.

Conversion is like the adrenaline-filled starting line in a footrace. The ability to begin this race against the Evil One is made possible because of salvation. It is filled with hope, anticipation, and excitement for what is to come. It is the moment where our lives come into focus and our purpose and path are made clear. It is that starting gunshot that lights a fire under our feet and sets our sights to one wholehearted and fully devoted pursuit. It is a powerful and empowering experience. In fact, our conversion ushers in the most powerful spiritual experience in our lives. Lunging forth in that first step begins the Christian race, building a foundation for our lives.

Some Christians, however, do not make it very far past the starting line; they fall into the temptation of trying to hold on to the "experience" of salvation or trying to recreate the feeling they had at their conversion through a worship service. Rather than looking forward to the plans and path God has for our lives, we spend our lives looking back at the initial spiritual high, thinking, *If only I could get back to that place, when I was close to God.*

This mind-set hamstrings us spiritually. This leads to remaining in the infancy of our faith, never maturing in our salvation, but this is not just an individual problem in each person's faith. The modern institutional church accelerates and often unknowingly trains and encourages this response from individuals through a corporate worship experience designed to try and recapture that spiritual high. Many modern churches emphasize the experience of worship, to the exclusion of the offering of our lives as worship.

Christians and churches are to commit to the difficult work of equipping the saints for the work of the ministry (Ephesians 4:12). Our purpose is to make disciples—training, challenging, and encouraging people to accept Jesus and grow in their faith. Church leaders can stymie spiritual growth if the entire content of every message, every Sunday, is an appeal to accept Jesus as Savior. Members of the congregation attend church each and every Sunday, hear about the need to accept Jesus as Savior, and, in some instances, are encouraged to make sure they have this essential experience correct in their lives. Members of the congregation, sensing that something is missing in their Christian lives, start to doubt their salvation and recommit to Christ, which translated means, "I will try harder."

They get trapped in cyclical Christianity, always finding themselves back at spiritual square one. They run as fast as they can in circles around the starting blocks but never progress. They are unequipped to push their faith to the limits because some leaders in churches fail to focus on strengthening the faith of individuals; rather, they draw them back each Sunday to question their salvation, out of fear that someone in the room is not really a Christian.

Some committed Christians are consistently faithful to witness to others about the need to repent, accept Jesus as Savior, and receive forgiveness for sins. This is fantastic, but if a Christian is only committed to seeing someone profess faith in Jesus and baptizing him or her, the fulfillment of the Great Commission is incomplete. Converts are never led to become disciples, leaving them in spiritual infancy.

Paul speaks to the church of the need to be weaned from spiritual milk and eat solid food (1 Corinthians 3:1–3). Because many have doubt placed on them every Sunday, never hearing messages of how to grow in Christ, they never get to live in the abundant life and in the joy of God. They keep revisiting their spiritual birth, evaluating its authenticity or trying to recapture the high of their conversion experience each week. They never take the first step into the spiritual battle raging all around them.

Paul had a tremendous conversion experience, but he didn't try to re-create it or re-experience it at any point during the rest of his life. Paul was focused on living his life as an offering of worship, as evidenced by seeing his life "being poured out as a drink offering" (2 Timothy 4:6). We can't be poured out as a drink offering if we aren't equipped to live.

The other bookend of the Christian life is eternal life. Some Christians always want to talk about the second coming and want to know when the rapture is going to take place. They want the prize, the finish line, but they want to do a running long-jump over real life, never exercising daily faith, and hang out at the finish line, waiting on death. They want to skip the hurdles faith demands and thereby lose the opportunity for spiritual victory. They are quick to begin a conversation with "I believe we are near the end times, don't you, pastor?" They talk about heaven as if it is going to make us into gods and goddesses.

I was in a church where a pianist played one of the most beautiful songs I have ever heard. A man, after hearing the song, went to the pulpit to lead in prayer and said, "I can't wait until I get to heaven. I will not have to suffer with any illness, I'll have no pain, and I will be perfect and able to play the piano just like that." Worship that overemphasizes the afterlife results in a worship experience of escape. Each worshiper becomes an island unto himself, seeking to enter an almost nirvana-type personal experience. Worship is not an escape; it is an engagement—an engagement with God and others.

Often, we use church, especially worship services, to escape the world, many times with the nodding approval of ministers who have carefully orchestrated the escape. God created us to tend to His creation by equipping us to engage the world, not to create an isolated counterculture. Rather, we are called to encounter the culture with the empowerment that comes from running with God in the race of faith. When we view worship as a means to escape the world, we often find ourselves in the middle of a Christian bubble, an exclusive Christian counterculture where only Christians feel welcomed and equipped with the proper lingo and expected emotional responses in order to participate. We guard the gates to our grand event, praising our champions and letting only the most spiritually fit compete.

Rather than running out into the world where many hurdles await, we escape to a comfortable arena that so often incites two responses from believers: (1) many believers misstep into competing with each other, rather than with the Evil One, using theology and biblical understanding as a measuring stick for spiritual fitness. They train to win debates rather than hearts; or (2) believers become spiritual cheerleaders or merely spectators, simply focused on celebrating each other and Jesus. They throw spiritual pep rallies full of praise, energy, affirmation, prayer, and music. They watch others run the race and listen to others' spiritual victories. They envision how they could run but never have the courage to enter the race because no one has ever taught them, demonstrated to them, or mentored them to observe the commands of Jesus.

These types of well-meaning, devoted, and wonderful people are legion in our churches. They are dedicated to the church as an organization, serving Jesus the best they know how and giving monetarily to its ministries, but they miss the best part of the race of faith because they have never been equipped to engage the world authentically, embodying Christ.

The role of corporate worship is not to emphasize any particular experience, whether it is to recapture the thrill of a past spiritual experience or to escape into an anticipated future experience. Worship is a lifelong act in which we engage, not merely a temporary involvement each Sunday morning. The reason we gather to worship is to focus on Jesus Christ and His sacrifice. This is what leads and inspires us to be transformed into His image. By commemorating and taking in His sacrifice, we are reminded to be a living sacrifice.

Christians "train to run; run to win." Paul speaks about obtaining victory by how we run or serve, how we engage the spiritual battle all around us. Our life of worship is the result of intentional preparation for an unavoidable struggle, not merely a sequence of unintentional and unplanned life events in which we lunge headfirst, naïve about the one we compete against, and hope for the best. We can't engage in a life of worship if we stay in the starting blocks or only long for the finish line.

A life offered as worship is the commitment to focus our complete energies as an expression of worship to the one true God, each and every day. This is how faith is lived out. How we run the race is the expression of faith that God honors. Worship is the ultimate expression of faith when it encompasses the full testimony of Scripture concerning worship. It puts it all on the line for Jesus because we are placing our confidence and trust in the teachings, commands, and promises that He spoke.

The worshiper doesn't interact with the people of this world on the world's terms, agenda, or ethics. We, the Christian worshipers, engage the people of this world on God's terms as individuals in the process of being transformed by Jesus Christ. This is how worship is an expression of faith. When laying our lives in their entirety—all of who we are—on the altar, our lives become our offerings of worship to God. This makes a bold statement that we believe in the sustaining power of Jesus Christ as we run toward the finish line. Jesus's life, death, and resurrection makes known the gospel of grace and love. The gospel of grace and love binds us and is expressed through our lives as we identify with Christ's complete sacrifice. This is the hope to change people's lives. This is the hope to fulfill the purpose of God in us.

Jesus taught that those who lose their lives for His sake will find them (Matthew 16:25). Identifying with Jesus in every aspect of our lives sets the stage for worship. Building our lives on Jesus, incorporating His character and commands into the spiritual fabric of who we are, is true worship. When we worship in spirit and in truth, we give a living testimony that we trust that Jesus is in us, and we are in Him as we take each step and live each day. We become the sweet aroma that is pleasing to God. We become the holy offering.

There are many implications and applications to the concept of "offered as worship." The first is that it doesn't lead us to withdraw from the world in fear of messing up. We engage the world with confidence, consecrating everything about ourselves for the purpose and will of God. We trust and we know that a life identified with His Son, Jesus Christ, will be accepted as worship.

The second implication of offering our lives as worship is that we find true freedom in Christ. Because we are expressing a changed life, we no longer have to try to impress God or others with our actions. Following the commands of Jesus and emulating His walk does not weigh us down with outside requirements but frees us to express our hearts—hearts connected to Jesus. We have been saved by Jesus, transformed by Jesus, and empowered by Jesus through the Holy

Spirit. Our lives become a true expression of what we have become in Christ, not doing things out of guilt or obligation. We get to worship Christ in spirit and truth—empowered and authentic, no deception, no hypocrisy. We worship in His Spirit and in His revelation.

The third implication is that in offering our full lives, we find peace in knowing that Jesus is our friend. He is present with us in everything we do. He blesses marriage and its intimacy by His presence, recreation and relaxation by His presence, parenting and its challenges by His presence, work and vocation by His presence, and church involvement by His presence, among other roles, relationships, and activities. He is with us at every turn, in every role in our lives, the living and present God, resurrecting our own sacrificed lives as new creations with Him. He accepts it all as worship to Him.

The fourth implication is that we find our validation from God and God alone. This is especially important when we face the promised persecution coming our way. We know that Jesus will be with us, giving us the strength to maintain faith. True and lasting validation cannot be obtained from other people, no matter what we purchase to impress them or how much we try to please them. This will ultimately lead to a wasted life and quite possibly to a life full of regrets and "what-ifs." A life offered as worship to God pleases Him, and that is the only validation we should seek. It is the ultimate use of what God has given us, just as it was for two of the three men in the parable of the talents—the two who invested the salvation they received. Our lives will never end in regret. If we invest our salvation and gifts in a life of worship, we will hear the words, "Well done, good and faithful slave. You were faithful with a few things, I will put you in charge of many things; enter into the joy of your master" (Matthew 25:21).

Offering our lives to God compels us to praise Jesus more and celebrate His wonderful work and name. We live faith in the race, in the struggle of life, between the starting line and finish line, with Christ as our companion and strength, seeking to extend the work of redemption through our lives. This is the abundant life—the chorus of life.

Join the Chorus

In chapter 1 of this book, I entitled a section "Beyond the Music." This was not meant to disparage music as we gather each Sunday morning to worship God. I emphasized that musical styles are not the most important thing in gathered worship. The important thing is the dedicated life that each worshipper brings to the experience of worship in a church service. Gathered worship is not to be our greatest expression of commitment to God. Nor is gathered worship the means we use to get the Spirit of God. Gathered worship is a celebration of the presence of God in the day-to-day living of our lives that took place the week before and committing to Him our day-to-day lives in the week to come.

We gather as a people to celebrate victories won in the fulfillment of the bold witness we have demonstrated through making disciples by going, baptizing, and teaching. We gather to equip others in order that they may be prepared to make disciples; and we gather to encourage those who didn't run as they were called to run. When these kinds of people gather for worship, with their lives in chorus with each other, we are ready for the music.

The music in worship becomes the harmony to an already present and strong melody of music that we sing through our daily actions. Gathered worship is the powerful expression of a committed people, each one dedicated to living each day for Jesus. The music becomes the powerful expression of our affection for God and His affection for us—the mutual embrace of the kindred spirits of people and God, enveloped in love. When we live each moment of life offered as worship, identified completely with Jesus's character and commands, believing His promises, and committed to fulfilling the entire Great Commission, we can proclaim with confidence and joy, worship is life.

AFTERWORD

Writing a book was not my original intention. *Offered*, or *Offered as Worship* was originally intended to be advanced through blogs, a website, and retreats, but I became uneasy with the original plan. I became convinced that "content" was needed. I spoke to my wife, children, Jacob Pierce, and others about it. They agreed that the above avenues would be more effective if a literary work set out the broad concepts of my thinking. So I began to write. Little did I know it would take more than two years to complete.

Romans 12:1–2 has been a central verse in my theology and ministry for years. The concept of offering our lives as sacrifices was something I had taught students for over two decades. I taught them that this was a part of worship. I taught students not to be conformed to the world, but to embrace transformation through the renewing of their minds. I failed, however, to comprehend the most powerful means to renew our minds and that was the commands of Jesus.

The Great Commission also has been a driving force in my theology and ministry. About six years ago I dissected the Great Commission as part of a personal devotion. As I studied the phrase "teaching them to observe all that I commanded you" (Matthew 28:20), I wrote down all the commands of Jesus that I could remember. I am embarrassed to say that I could not recall fifteen from the dozens of them recorded in the Gospels. As I studied these commands what I realized was that I had not developed a synthesized view between personal spiritual transformation as described by Jesus and Paul and my call to reach other people with the gospel and disciple them.

I concluded that the observance of the commands was essential to personal transformation. They re-order our perspectives of God, people, and the world. When I began to see that these commands were the avenue to present our "bodies a living and holy sacrifice", I saw their centrality to living a life of worship. If they were to be grafted into every part of my life it would leave no part of my life outside the expression of worship to God—as a living sacrifice.

I chose to make the book largely devotional in nature. It covers a lot of theological ground. It is a summary of some essential teachings, doctrines, habits, and traits. There is much more to say and it will most likely be said. The conclusions come from a simple, straightforward interpretation of Scripture. I chose to use stories of people who influenced my life instead of historical examples as illustrations because I want to show that everyday acts of worship through ordinary people have an impact.

It will take some time, possibly three years or more, to incorporate Jesus's teachings and commands into life—into ours and the lives of those we mentor. Interestingly, this is roughly the same amount of time Jesus spent with His disciples in order to equip them. The commands are something we have to "live with" for a while. My hope is it will birth in you what it has begun to bring forth in my life and that is the ability to live in the freedom of worship. It truly is refreshing to know that my worship isn't confined to doing "religious" things and that my *offered* life is accepted by God.

If you want to explore further how to offer your life as worship, more resources will be available at www.OfferedAsWorship.com. I hope you will find them helpful.

With regards,
Bill

ABOUT THE AUTHOR

Bill has served in campus ministry since 1988. He has been senior campus minister at the University of Alabama at Birmingham since 1999. Bill strives to equip students to live a bold life: an offering of worship that resonates with the teachings of Jesus. Bill is a native of Oklahoma where he earned a Bachelor of Music from Oklahoma Baptist University. He went on to earn his Master of Divinity and Doctor of Ministry degrees. Bill preaches frequently in churches in the Birmingham area and has served several churches as interim. He loves baseball, college football, and the outdoors. He serves his community as president of the youth baseball association. Bill and his wife, Sheri Jones Morrison, have been married 24 years. They have four children: Caroline, Annelise, Victoria, and William.